A Handbook of Theory for Social Care:

Volume Two

By: Iain Maclean, Siobhan Maclean
and Lee Pardy-McLaughlin

Kirwin Maclean Associates

A Handbook of Theory for Social Care: Volume Two
By Iain Maclean, Siobhan Maclean and Lee Pardy-McLaughlin

First published 2007 by Kirwin Maclean Associates
First Edition 2007: *ISBN-13:   978-1-903575-43-7*

A catalogue record for this book will be available from the British Library.

Printed in Great Britain by Kirwin Maclean Associates

CONTENTS

INTRODUCTION

In Volume One of this two volume series, we started the introduction by saying that the reader should not be intimidated by the word 'theory'. The same sentiment applies equally to this volume.

The intention of this volume (like Volume One) is to demystify some of the language that has built up around specific theories. Theories themselves must connect to life since they seek to explain life, behaviours, situations etc. Arguably, theories have become complex because life is complex. In trying to explain the diversity of human responses to similar situations, theories have developed their own 'branches'. An academic or writer may focus on one element of a theory, at the expense of other aspects of the same theory, to explain why some people respond in certain ways.

Whenever you are considering theory, we would urge you to:

- recognise that no single theory can explain everything: When a person engages in an action (or inaction) the reason for their behaviour can be rooted in a range of causes or motives.
- related to the first point, recognise that some theoretical approaches just don't work with some people. Applying Brief Solution Focussed Therapy can be really effective with some people. For other people, it leaves them cold.
- take a critical approach to theory. If it doesn't "work", why not? Can you adapt aspects such that it is helpful?
- Always apply the value base to theory – much of the theory in this volume is drawn from outside of social care/social work practice. Theory may have its roots in education, psychology or management. As such, it may not incorporate social care values and you should take responsibility for applying these
- And finally, never be intimidated by theory. You use it every day.

One of the intentions of Volume Two is to give the reader an understanding of the more complex theories, models or perspectives in social care or social work. There is therefore only limited overlap with Volume One.

If the theory, model or perspective you are looking for is not in this volume, it is probably in Volume One. To clarify this, a list of the contents of Volume One appears as Appendix 1 (page 157).

In this volume, there is direction about where the reader can go to from here. As previously stated, theories develop branches or 'schools' and they evolve. We would encourage you to pursue the theories that are most relevant to you.

This volume concludes with a section on the application of theory to practice. This section should help you to see the way that theory impacts on your work on a day to day basis.

SECTION ONE: ANTI-OPPRESSIVE PRACTICE

This is intentionally the first section in this book. We come from the position that all practice in social care and social work should be underpinned by a commitment to anti-oppressive practice. The first section in Volume One explored some of the key processes in oppression and some of the theories relating to challenging oppression. In this volume, we are looking more specifically at theories and models in this area.

Reading this section you will learn more about:

- The PCS model
- Social constructionism
- Social and medical perspectives
- Discourse analysis
- The feminist perspective
- The black perspective

FURTHER READING

This handbook provides an introduction to the main theories of social care. For further, more detailed information on the areas covered in this section, see the following:

- Banks, S. (2001) *Ethics and Values in Social Work.* Second Edition. (Basingstoke) Palgrave.

- Barnes, C. and Mercer, G. (2003) *Disability.* (Cambridge) Policy Press.

- Beckett, C. and Maynard, A. (2005) *Values and Ethics in Social Work: An Introduction.* (London) SAGE.

- Dominelli, L. (1997) *Anti-Racist Social Work.* (Basingstoke) Palgrave.

- Dominelli, L. (2002) *Anti-oppressive Social Work Theory and Practice.* (Basingstoke) Palgrave.

- Dominelli, L. (2002) *Feminist Social Work Theory and Practice.* (Basingstoke) Palgrave.

- Martin, E. and Martin, J. (1995) *Social Work and the Black Experience.* NASW Press.

- Parton, N and O'Byrne, P. (2000) *Constructive Social Work: Towards a New Practice.* (Basingstoke) MacMillan.

- Swain, J., French, S., Thomas, C. and Barnes, C. (Eds) (2004) *Disabling Barriers, Enabling Environments.* (London) Sage.

- Thompson, N. (2005) *Anti-Discriminatory Practice.* Third Edition. (Basingstoke) Palgrave.

PCS MODEL

Developed by Thompson (eg: 2005) the PCS Model offers a method to analyse the way that oppression operates and how it impacts on service users. The model proposes three levels (P, C and S as follows) which closely relate to each other.

P – personal or psychological
C – cultural
S – structural

This model basically provides a framework and gives a language to much of what we explored in Section 1 of Volume One.

Personal/Psychological

This basically refers to individual oppression – where an individual's thoughts, attitudes and actions sustain a broader pattern of discrimination.

Thompson explains that the P also refers to prejudice and practice – in that an individual worker's practice will reflect their personal views and their prejudices.

Cultural

Thompson explores the way that groups share common values, based on which they reach a consensus about what is "normal". Conformity to these constructed social norms is expected by groups. Where people don't conform, they may be segregated by the 'group'.

Thompson also outlines the way that comedy/comic humour is used to maintain these norms – as we covered in Volume One humour is often used as a mechanism of oppression.

Structural

Thompson states that there are a range of structural social divisions which are closely related to power dynamics. Within society oppression is *"sewn in"* at an institutional level within the detail of society. Thompson refers to wider social forces and the socio-political dimension of the way difference is viewed by society.

Thompson proposes a diagrammatic representation of the model, as follows:

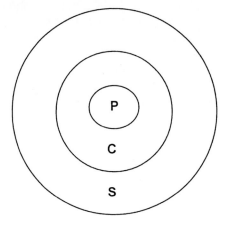

This is designed to show the way that personal prejudicial feelings are deeply embedded within cultural influences and structural forces. Hence personal oppression is reliant on cultural groupings and structural forces, whilst structural forces and cultural norms would not be upheld without personal prejudices.

Basically this model gives an explanation of the strength of oppression and the processes of socialisation and internalisation as covered in Volume One. It can be useful to help explore the nature of the oppression faced by service users. It is only in understanding the oppression that a worker can seek to challenge this.

Many of the theories covered in the remainder of this section build on the PCS model. For example, constructionist approaches explore the way that social norms are constructed (as in the C of the PCS model).

SOCIAL CONSTRUCTIONISM

Like all theories, the heart of social constructionism is quite simple, but it has quickly developed a language that is itself a barrier to understanding.

Social constructionism highlights a basic truth that most societal views are generated by people (social) and then applied through the activity of public services and other organisations (constructed). One of the consequences of this is that views and opinions can change and so the way that society orders itself can also change.

It is probably best to give examples of this. For many years Chris Phillipson has argued that old age is constructed by the capitalist system (e.g.: 1998).

In the 1980s when there was high unemployment and it appeared that this would remain, there was talk of retirement starting at age 60 for most people. This was partly so that the unemployment figures could be reduced. However once the state became aware of the increasing longevity of people and the implications this would have for state funding then the debate turned the opposite way. The state retirement age has been raised to 65 for women (to be the same as men) and it is likely that the state pension age will rise to 68 in the UK within the next 30 years or so.

The age at which someone should retire from work is not "naturally determined". As a society we decide. We will decide as a result of consideration of various factors such as the cost to society (and us!)

The current role of carers in society could be viewed as socially constructed. Social care services have only ever supported a minority of people who needed support. Most adults with learning disabilities have always lived in the community. Even when institutional care was at its height in the 1960s only about 5% (at most) of adults with a learning disability lived in an institution. Ninety five percent of adults with a learning disability lived with family, a partner or got along by themselves.

As the 1980s and 1990s progressed, the numbers of people, who needed care and support (older people, people with mental health problems, people with learning disabilities), was noticeably increasing. The possibility arose that demand for residential care would balloon and this would involve huge costs to society. One response of society (mainly expressed through the government) was to create a group of people known as carers. A carer is a family member or friend of the person who needs care who provides that care without being paid. Over the last 15 years or so carers have been defined in terms of their role and have been given some rights (limited rights admittedly).

The subtext to the creation of the role of carer is that if people with care needs are adequately cared for by the family member (carer) then the person with care needs will not need residential care (or will not need residential care for several years) and so the state is saved the cost of funding a huge number of residential care placements.

Childhood is another concept that is socially constructed. There are still many older people alive today who left school at 14 or 15 and started work.

The age of consent for sex was only raised to 16 in the 1880s, before then it was 14. There are many societies that allow young women to marry at 14 or so. The Netherlands moved the age of consent for sex down to 14 in the 1990s.

In the UK there has been a movement to protect and extend childhood until the young person celebrates their 18th birthday. One example of this is the law relating to abuse of trust. This law makes it an offence for a teacher or care worker to have sexual contact with a 16 or 17 year old they are in day to day contact with through work.

The social construction of health and social care can also be seen in the way the main ethos and focus of our work has changed. Until the1960s the role of health and social care services that were involved with people with mental health problems, people with learning disabilities and people with physical disabilities was to act as agents of social control.

People with such care needs (children and adults) were placed in large institutions. They were congregated together, segregated from society. Society comforted itself by saying "they're best with their own" and "they wouldn't be able to cope in society". Crudely put – care staff were social police. In the 1950s some of the long stay learning disability hospitals had individuals in them who were so independent and so aware of their detention that they escaped. Some evaded recapture.

As a result of various developments the focus of social care has moved from agent of social control to empowerment of service users. What a turn around! This has been as a result of protests from service users (arguably people with physical disabilities have been prominent, but all social care groups have been involved in promoting their rights). Additionally carers have often expressed the rights of their loved ones for a decent, ordinary life. There have also been professionals who have been prominent in wanting services to improve.

Social constructionists would raise various questions, such as:

Are we really empowering people or are we better at hiding the fact that we are still agents of social control?

This question is most relevant to mental health services and childrens services, but there are times when it applies to all social care services.

It is also particularly relevant when the question of race and ethnicity is added. Mental health services have singularly failed to shake off institutional racism. The number of African Caribbean men who are compulsory detained is disproportionately high compared to white men who are compulsory detained.

There have been significant changes in social care in the last 40 years. What of the next 40 years? Which way will future changes go? At present social care and social work are being pulled into other professional areas. Children's care services are being pulled into education. How long will this last? There are competing pressures – firstly for more individual care, secondly the cost of care is rising, the cost of individualised care is huge. Could this be resolved by community involvement? Technology and robotics? Could the role of social worker be reserved for the most vulnerable (reinforcing the sense of stigma associated with having a social worker)? Will the articulate middle classes arrange social care services for themselves or their loved ones in the same way they book a package holiday on the internet? Self assessment is already being piloted in some parts of England with people who have low level care needs. In effect people who self assess can refer themselves on to the key professional (e.g.: occupational therapist) without the need for a social worker. Hence, whatever state social care and social work are at now, it is important to recognise they will change in the years ahead.

Language

The social constructionist perspective emphasises that language is a major tool. The development of the term carer is just one example. Beckett (2006) points out that much social work and social care activity focuses on problems, needs and risks. There is an air of negativity and burden about the way service users are discussed.

The pressure for social care and social work staff to be negative about service users has increased in recent years. Eligibility criteria (the threshold which must be reached before services are agreed) have been introduced (and raised higher) resulting in staff emphasising how difficult the behaviour of a person is or how significant a person's care needs are etc, in order to access resources.

In Volume One, we discussed the links between language and social imagery and the way that language can be dehumanising. This theme is central to social constructionism. One clear example is the way that the language used to describe key needs can be dehumanising. For example, regular reference is made to service users needing "feeding" or within assessment and care planning documentation questions are asked about "feeding". Feeding is a word we generally use in conjunction with animals (feeding time at the zoo) or babies. Most adults "eat". They do not "feed themselves". However, in relation to people in receipt of social and health care, language changes – people are dehumanised and effectively negative social roles are constructed.

Self Narrative/Self Perception

Social constructionists also emphasise the importance of self narrative. The person with mental health problems who stops taking medication can be viewed by professionals as not complying with their care plan. The service user's view may be that the medication has pervasive side effects that reduces their quality of life. Childrens services are increasingly open to how teenagers view their experience of being "looked after". However both these examples illustrate that there are limitations. If the mental health service user stops taking their medication and then commits suicide, or the teenager wants to stay out till all hours and is then at significant risk. After a point, services have to be pragmatic, regardless of the theoretical perspective.

There are situations where a social constructionist perspective could be applied but isn't. An example could be the older person who quietly but clearly says they want to remain in their own home even if they hardly move from their chair for risk of falling. Still social workers can listen to the son or daughter express their anxiety and then see the older person brow beaten into attending a day centre or even entering residential care.

It is an old saying that in history the winners write the history books. In social care and social work, we need to avoid the situation where the assessment is entirely the viewpoint of the assessor. In social care and social work we must avoid the person being described solely by family members and professionals. The service user's perspective must be acknowledged. It is to be seen if it can then be acted on.

The Application of Social Constructionism

Often concepts of constructionism are presented very academically and staff struggle to see how this theory may apply to their everyday work. However, there are potentially a number of basic but useful applications. For example, staff should:

- Use anti-oppressive language which promotes dignity and respect
- Question "reality". When presented with a problem/issue etc. staff shouldn't necessarily accept this as fact. Whose reality is this? How is the problem defined or constructed?
- Where a person tells you they "should" do something, question why? People should not feel under pressure from social norms, as this can lead to a curtailment of choices.
- Encourage people to express their feelings and adopt a "narrative" approach (this is further covered in section 3).
- Listen to service users and carers.

SOCIAL AND MEDICAL PERSPECTIVES

Social constructionists acknowledge that realities are constructed in a range of ways. The "realities" which health professionals hold may be very different to those of social care professionals. In many ways, this builds on an understanding of the social and medical model which we introduced in Volume One.

With an increased emphasis on joint working, it is helpful to have a clear understanding of the impact of social and medical perspectives on service users situations. These are sometimes referred to as the social discourse and the medical discourse – where discourse is essentially about which one is most influential (see pages 31-32 for further information).

Within every branch of social care with children and adults social and medial perspectives each put forward their own interpretation of why a person is in the situation they are.

The medical perspective locates the difficulty within the individual; they have an illness (physical or mental), an impairment or a type of personality that results in them being in the situation they are in. Through medical intervention the person can be cured or their difficulties lessened. Identification (diagnosis) of the illness or condition is by a doctor who also knows the cure.

The social perspective views the problems as located within society or the environment. One of the tenets of the social perspective is to argue that there is diversity within the human condition (e.g.: disability, sexual orientation, mental health). This diversity is to be celebrated and embraced, not treated.

Disability

It is in the area of disability that, arguably, the social perspective has had the greatest success in displacing the medical perspective.

For most of the Twentieth century, the medical perspective was the dominant discourse in the care of people with a disability. People with physical disabilities and people with learning disabilities were diagnosed by doctors and if they couldn't be cared for in the family home were placed in services called hospitals which were staffed by nurses and doctors. In these hospitals some research was conducted which today would be considered voyeuristic and intrusive. The weaknesses of the medical perspective were progressively exposed. Behind the medical perspective was a body and health 'fascism'. The perfect body and mind and ideal health was held in awe. Deviation from this ideal was considered abnormal. Darwin's evolutionary theory was also 'hijacked' and used to argue that nations and races must encourage the fittest and most intelligent to reproduce. Only the fittest nation will survive. If a nation allows people who do not meet the 'ideal' to reproduce, the nation will be swamped and it will lose out against other nations. This was the eugenics movement. One consequence of the eugenics movement was that the rights of adults with disabilities to have relationships and to have children was casually and comprehensively violated. Although we are beginning to develop our understanding, the secret history of the enforced sterilisation of women with learning disabilities has still to be fully exposed (although we do know a lot.)

The social model has argued that the diagnosis of individuals with a label or condition is largely irrelevant. It often told us nothing about how the person should be treated (which is that every person with a disability should be treated like any individual with human rights). The diagnosis and labelling was therefore a distraction, it highlighted difference (in a negative way). The striving for an answer to the question "What is the cause of the person's disability?" was also often empty. Of all people with a learning disability, between 40 to 60% have no identifiable cause or diagnosis.

Crucially the social perspective of disability illustrated how society was ordered for the benefit of ambulant people who can hear and have no visual impairment. With the advent of the car, it became clear that society could structure itself according to its own priorities. Buildings are designed so cars could smoothly get to the six floor (multi story car parks). But a person in a wheelchair was fortunate to get through the front door of a building, let alone onto the sixth floor.

If society wants to, it can arrange itself so that all people are included. By making so much of social life inaccessible to people with disabilities, society was unconsciously conveying that people with disabilities are not important.

In the last ten to fifteen years there has been significant improvement. Buildings are now far more accessible, access to public transport has improved and facilities to aid communication for people who are deaf have also improved. In general, attitudes to the inclusion of people with disabilities in society have also moved in the right direction. This is not to say that we have achieved the ideal society. People with disabilities are still at increased risk of unemployment (and consequently poverty) and of poorer health outcomes than non disabled people. There has been an improvement but more still needs to be done.

The disability movement also conveyed the need to respect diversity. People with a physical disability do not claim that their disability makes them better than non disabled people. It is the way the person is and all people have a right to be respected for the way they are.

Sexual Orientation

In 1992 the World Health Organisation finally removed homosexuality as a medical diagnosis from their classifications. Recently some medical research suggests that there may be a biological basis for some people being homosexual. However the medical perspective in the 1960s (male homosexual sexual activity was illegal until 1967) was that homosexuality was a treatable illness. Individuals were subjected to aversion treatment regimes intended to 'cure' the person of their homosexuality. Even after male homosexual sexual activity was made lawful, medical 'treatment' programmes were still available.

The gay and lesbian community has made clear their right to live their lives as they wish to. The call to respect diversity has been given significant support with the societal move towards equality for all.

Attention Deficit Hyper-Activity Disorder (ADHD)

One of the more recent areas of debate around the social and medical models has been caused by the increasing diagnosis of children with ADHD. There is an established professional view that ADHD is a definable medical condition which is treatable by medication and management techniques by parents and teachers.

From the medical perspective, there is a list of symptoms that a doctor will ask the parents to comment on. A child would need to exhibit symptoms to an extent that is unusual for a child of that age, for a period of six months. Symptoms include:

- Fails to pay close attention to detail or makes careless errors in work or play
- Fails to follow through instructions or to finish homework or chores
- Disorganised about tasks and activities
- In young children, runs around or excessively climbs over things
- In adolescence, has feelings of restlessness
- Fidgets with hands or feet or squirms on seat
- Fails to wait in line or fails to wait turns in games or groups
- Interrupts or intrudes on others

Doctors argue that in children diagnosed with ADHD there are often other problems:

- 60% have confrontational defiant behaviour (the child argues and refuses to comply with adults)
- learning difficulties, e.g.: dyslexia
- Clinical depression (in about 30% of children diagnosed with ADHD)
- Anxiety disorders (in about 30% of children diagnosed with ADHD)

There is no clear cause for ADHD. The child's temperament and genetic factors have been suggested. Diagnosis is made by a doctor after consultation with the parents and the child. The doctor may also involve psychologist, health visitors etc.

Treatment could involve medication. Ritalin is probably the most well known but there are others. As with all medications and their use by children, there is concern within the medical community that it should not be used for indefinite periods.

Management techniques are also frequently recommended and are focussed on a behavioural approach:

- Establish boundaries about behaviour and have a daily routine for the child
- Be consistent in the handling of the child
- Use rewards to reinforce good behaviour
- Use sanctions for unacceptable behaviour

From the social perspective, various questions are raised about ADHD:

- The diagnosis of ADHD is a clinical diagnosis. This means a doctor draws together all the information and makes a best (informed) guess. There is no definable, definite marker for ADHD. There is no blood test, no scan, no X-ray that can detect ADHD. The doctor is particularly reliant on the parent's viewpoint.
- It appears that many children with the diagnosis of ADHD are in families where there is a history of domestic violence. Some of the symptoms of post-traumatic stress disorder and the symptoms of ADHD are similar (e.g.: effects on ability to concentrate). The social perspective argues that the effects of domestic violence on a child are significant
- Many children with the diagnosis of ADHD are in families where the parents have not created and sustained strong attachments with the child. Therefore the child could be displaying attachment anxieties.
- It appears that in the last twenty years parental concern about how dangerous the world is outside the family home has meant that children have been brought into the home. The main parental anxieties are around roads and the perceived risk of child abduction and murder. If this is true (that children are not allowed to play out as much as in the 1960s) then children have to expend their energy in the home rather than run around outside.
- It is not clear if there is any social economic influence on the prevalence of children diagnosed with ADHD. Are children diagnosed with ADHD disproportionately drawn from poor families?
- Following diagnosis of ADHD one of the principle interventions is management techniques. This is code for applying good parenting practice. If good parenting practice 'cures' a child of ADHD then is it really a medical problem?

The social perspective towards ADHD raises questions rather than promotes a cast iron alternative. It is possible that some children are rightly diagnosed with ADHD. The social perspective would certainly raise concerns about the increasingly common use of the diagnosis and ask is it, at times, being used inappropriately?

Mental Health

Arguably, it is in the area of mental health that the social and medical perspectives have had the most significant debate.

The traditional medical perspective has a certain strength in its claims of clinically definable diagnosis. There are specific patterns of behaviour and expressed emotional states that can be given a specific diagnosis. The definable conditions include:

- Schizophrenia
- Bi polar Disorder (formerly called Manic Depression)
- Depression
- Personality Disorders
- Anxiety Disorders

The medical perspective would argue that many mental health conditions are caused by metabolic or chemical imbalances in the brain. The chemical imbalances result in the brain's functioning being adversely effected and altering the person's perceptions of contact with people and in some cases, generating perceptions of voices or events that other people (who do not have the mental health condition) do not experience. In general the medical perspective would claim that most conditions can be treated. Treatment could include a range of interventions. The most 'medical' being medication. However, other treatments are available and could include talking treatments (such as counselling or psychotherapy and cognitive behavioural therapy) and opportunities to find mutual support from self help groups etc.

As always in the medical perspective, much of the power rests with professionals, especially the doctor. Within mental health services this power is confirmed by the role given to doctors in terms of decision making in the Care Programme Approach and potentially, if doctors feel there is a need to compulsorily detain a person with mental health needs, they can recommend this.

The social perspective has been developed in the last thirty years or so. Many people have contributed to this development which has many aspects.

One of the points raised by the social perspective on mental health is to highlight that the diagnosis of mental health conditions is not as scientific as diagnosis for physical medical conditions. In terms of physical health and illnesses, there are often identified patterns of symptoms and clear 'markers' e.g.: results of a blood test. There are no reliable biological markers for schizophrenia or other mental health conditions (Stenfert Kroese et al 2001, Pam 1995). Doctors have still not established that there are verifiable physiological differences between people diagnosed with schizophrenia and those not diagnosed. There are no tests or scans that can show a person 'has' schizophrenia, depression or bi-polar disorder (Stenfert Kroese et al 2001). Arguably more concerning is that no psychological or behavioural markers have been discovered which differentiate people diagnosed as having schizophrenia from people who have not been diagnosed without creating unacceptable proportions of false positives and false negatives (Sarbin 1990). This is because lots of people 'hear voices' and engage in a range of behaviours but that does not mean we, automatically, have schizophrenia.

The listed symptoms for schizophrenia are so many that two people may both be diagnosed as having schizophrenia but not share any of the same symptoms. Therefore why claim that the two people have the same 'illness'. Stenfert Kroese et al (2001) point out that these concerns were first raised in the early 1960s and have not been laid to rest. Psychiatric diagnosis is based on the doctor interviewing the patient. It is a clinical diagnosis. This is a posh term for best guess, although doctors would argue it is a well educated and informed guess.

The meaning of anxiety and depression has been contested for many years. Smail (1984 and 1987) has argued that far from being a mental illness, that anxiety and depression are often rational (although unconscious) responses to a person's lived experiences.

Smail (1984 and 1987) argued that anxiety and conditions like agoraphobia are responses to the individual's perception that they are being continually judged and that the judgement finds them to have failed to be good enough. In this the person's anxiety or agoraphobia is a blinding, truthful insight. We are never slim enough, good looking enough, earning enough money, etc as demanded by society. Therefore the sense of anxiety or the avoidance of going out is a rational (but unconscious) response.

Social perspectives on depression follow a similar theme. If a person is in a deeply unsatisfactory relationship, if they are being abused, if they are isolated and/or are in a constant state of grinding poverty is it any surprise they become depressed? Depression is often characterised by low mood, poor motivation, broken sleep patterns (difficulty getting to sleep and difficulty getting up). Again Smail (1984 and 1987) argued that depression is a rational (unconscious) response to the person's lived situation. The person is deeply unhappy. It is not surprising the person has difficulty getting up or difficulty with motivation since they have nothing to look forward to that day.

If some mental health conditions are a response to a person's situation, then the use of medication raises various questions. One of the main points is that the medication will not alter the life difficulties the person is facing and that these life difficulties could be the cause of the person's mental health problems.

By diagnosing a person with, say, depression when the cause of the depression is an abusive relationship or poverty etc, then the individual is being cast into the 'sick' role. Arguably the person is not sick at all. The environment the person is having to live in is 'sick' and so this should be addressed.

Social perspectives on mental health have been further developed by discussions about cultural sensitivity. Many of the 'markers' used by doctors in diagnosis can be viewed in culturally specific ways. So that, for example, what is viewed as an inappropriate response in one culture can be viewed as entirely appropriate in another culture.

Medication

The social perspective continues to raise concerns about aspects of medication. One of the concerns is that people in residential care or health settings are at risk of having higher levels of drugs, larger cocktails of drugs (termed polypharmacotherapy) and to be on drugs for longer than people who have care needs but who live with family or independently in the community.

The side effects of psychotropic medication are well known. Some people taking certain types of drugs in the long term will suffer from permanent neurological damage. This could effect the way they walk and how they present (facial expression). There is still continuing debate about the effectiveness of medication such as antipsychotic drugs. Antipsychotic drugs are used to treat people diagnosed with schizophrenia. Confusingly, some of these drugs are also termed neuroleptic.

Doctors would point out that newer drugs have fewer side effects. Also the use of drugs enables many people with mental health problems to function in the community (which would not have been possible before the development of a range of medications).

Medication and Challenging Behaviour

Care staff who work with individuals whose behaviour is a challenge to them appear to readily welcome a doctor who offers medication as a response to the service user's challenging behaviour. This is partly because so many non-medical staff see the doctor as the expert, but what about the service user? They know more than anyone the effect the medication has on them. Non medical staff also appear to believe the medication will 'cure' the service user. In respect of addressing behaviour which is a challenge, sometimes medication acts as a chemical cosh. When the service user is subdued (de facto) then life is easier for staff.

There is increasing evidence about the effectiveness of non-aversive interventions for people with learning disabilities and challenging behaviour (Fleming and Stenfert Kroese 1993). Such approaches require a committed team, but too many care staff appear in awe of the promises (spoken or unspoken) that medication offers. When it comes to addressing challenging behaviour, it is not clear that the promises of medication are fulfilled.

The 'awe' that care staff have towards medicine partly accounts for why people with social care needs who are in residential care are at increased risk of being on higher levels of medication and for longer periods compared to people living in their own home or the family home.

Diversity

People with mental health problems have been at the forefront of promoting the social perspective. One point that has been made is that some of the experiences of people with mental health problems are an expression of the variety that occurs in the human condition. An example is that some people hear voices. If the person finds a way to live with the voices, then why the need for medical or other interventions.

Balancing the Social and Medical Perspectives in Mental Health

The vast majority of doctors would argue that the use of medication to treat people with mental health problems is essential to continue the progress made in treating people in the community.

It has to be acknowledged that the behaviour and mental health problems of some people, at certain times of their life, is so unusual and can result in such significant self harm (and very occasionally harm to others) that there needs to be significant intervention and this has a significant medical aspect to it.

Whilst some mental health service user groups see suicide as a human right, we would also align ourselves with the medical perspective that suicide should be prevented wherever possible.

There have been some aspects of a coming together. Many doctors are more willing to enter into a discussion with the service user about what medication may be best for them, what side effects the person is presently experiencing and what strength the medication should be.

Many service users are willing to take their medication if they feel they have been involved in discussing the prescription in the first place and if they are confident that their doctor will respond if the present medication causes any problems.

Many doctors are also conscious of the service user's wider needs, including social networks, meaningful occupation or contribution to society as well as the importance of basic needs such as housing.

Drug and Alcohol Dependency

The social perspective on drug and alcohol dependency would argue that attention needs to be paid to the social and relationship difficulties that a person has experienced that have resulted in them taking drugs or alcohol.

Addressing the original problems or addressing the service user's perception of the original problems should result in the service user starting to regain a sense of control in their life which will enable them to regain control of their substance use.

The medical perspective would argue that where a person has been consuming significant amounts of drugs or alcohol for five years or so, then a physiological addiction has been established. There has been such a significant change in the brain that the person has a genuine physiological craving for the substance if the person stops consuming it. The compulsion to have a drink or a 'fix' becomes stronger as more is consumed.

The craving to have drugs or alcohol therefore develops a momentum of its own. Also the slide into dependency may, or may not, have been due to personal and social difficulties. However, the strength of the addiction creates difficulties because the individual could lose their job, spend all their finances on drug or alcohol use, and their social network could collapse about them as they steal money from family and are absorbed in the need to feed their addiction.

Chaotic drug or alcohol use is characterised by social irresponsibility since the physiological addiction is so strong. Once a person's drug or alcohol use has become so chaotic, then the rehabilitation (abstinence) approach is to bring together aspects of the social and the medical model.

The abstinence approach accepts the medical model view on physiological addiction. Therefore all intake of drugs must be stopped from the point a person joins an abstinence programme. To assist the service user and to convey that if they consume drugs or alcohol they will be found out, many programmes have daily breathalyser tests and urine tests. Sometimes the taking of urine samples is observed. This is felt necessary since otherwise the service user could bring in someone else's urine since their own craving to relapse is so strong.

Abstinence programmes provide information on the effects long term addictions have on the brain. Service users on abstinence programmes also have to consider what they have lost as a result of their addiction. Such programmes are often group work based and draw both on group work theory and cognitive behavioural theory (motivational interviewing).

The abstinence approach draws together the medical and social perspectives by being clear about the physiological addiction the person has but stating that it is the individual's responsibility to refuse to take drugs or have alcohol. The abstinence approach prepares the person for how difficult abstaining will be (explains why it's so difficult) and provides strategies to uphold their responsibility to abstain.

Application to Practice

Understanding medical and social perspectives and associated processes is vital in terms of joint working situations. It is also important to acknowledge that the perspectives are exactly that – perspectives – not necessarily fact and reality. Just as the constructionist approach would argue, we would encourage staff to question concepts and perhaps use the "best" of each approach to support work with service users.

DISCOURSE ANALYSIS

Discourse analysis (or critical analysis) is a way of questioning that seeks to identify the assumptions that social relations are based on.

Discourse analysis has been used in many disciplines. Traditionally, one of the main uses has been in the field of linguistics, where discourse analysis has been used to analyse language and text. It is an approach that studies the organisation of language not in grammatical terms so much, as the broader source, use or intention of language. The social context of the language and the interaction that is generated are important parts of the whole analysis.

In the social sciences, discourse analysis has been used to deconstruct the use of language. Since everything has to be described in some way (language or text is used), then this means that everything can be deconstructed by the use of discourse analysis.

Arguably, discourse analysis is a very academic activity. Within some of the disciplines that use discourse analysis, the language used is very esoteric (understandable only to an 'in' club of people).

All Social Structures and Relations are Socially Created

The rise of discourse analysis is partly due to the ending of the view that there is some established ordering or meaning in the human world. Post modernism has the view that all societies and all relationships are socially constructed (humans, in some ways, decide how they wish to arrange society).

The ordering of society is not based on a 'natural' structure or universal truth. Once people have created a social system, this then becomes rooted and established. Its legitimacy is asserted through various claims (language). All these claims can be analysed and questioned. The motivations of people (others and ourselves) should be identifiable through discourse analysis. One of the assumptions of discourse analysis is that all social perceptions are subjective and that dominant social perceptions (or beliefs) are just expressions of the dominant discourses that are able to exert influence or control over society at that time. There is no intrinsic, absolute truth.

Discourse analysis is not intended to establish a new answer. It is seeking to reveal the underlying assumptions, motives and politics that are located within and around language, text and social relations.

Discourse Analysis and Politics

Some of the very fertile fields for discourse analysis (although it is now used in numerous fields) are those of politics, social policy and ideology. These fields are profoundly dependent on language and text and so open themselves to an analysis of their discourses (discussions, claims or arguments).

One example is the contribution of elite racism to institutional racism in Western Europe. Discourse analysis has been used to explain how elites are able to maintain dominant discourses through the media, political propaganda, business policies, advertising etc. Parliamentary debates focus on "illegal" immigration (these concepts could be broken down themselves by discourse analysis). The dominant discourses focus on claims of the problems immigrants create, the threat to 'our' culture and the cost to 'us'. The dominant discourse focuses on the alleged harm done to us and fails to make any acknowledgement of the problems experienced by immigrants caused by institutions in the UK. The pervasiveness of the dominant discourse can be expressed by discourse analysis. Additionally, the limited in-roads that anti-racist discourses have made compared to very recent anti-terrorist discourses which subtly (and not so subtly) re-enforce racist discourses, illustrates the dominance of elitist discourses.

Application to Practice

Discourse analysis, at its most helpful, can aid in the breaking down of cultural assumptions and make clear the societal power biases that oppress minorities. At its most esoteric, some of the language is almost impenetrable and is mainly of use to academics pursuing academic debates.

FEMINIST PERSPECTIVE

There is no one Feminist Theory! Rather there has been development of a range of perspectives and points which have been loosely grouped together. These perspectives have shared values which include:-

- a recognition of the extensive inequalities in society based on gender with men consistently being dominant
- the need to be woman focused and the recognition that a glib gender blind approach won't work
- it isn't just a case of promoting more women into management posts. The sources of power and the construction of hierarchies should be questioned themselves
- related to this is the social construction of male dominance, especially in the use of language but also in gender roles more broadly
- a recognition of the diversity of women's experience. The experience of black women, disabled women and gay women has been different from white heterosexual women

The Impact of Feminist Arguments

Given the variety of feminist viewpoints it is possibly helpful to point out some of the success of the feminist movement.

- Feminism has successfully highlighted the extensiveness of domestic violence and has campaigned for violence on women partners to be seen in the same way as violence in the street on a stranger. Amazingly, until the mid 1990s a husband could not be accused of raping his wife even though rape in marriage in the UK, was a daily occurrence.

The development of the women's aid movement and refuges has been a key aspect of liberating women from violent oppression.

- The power of language and the importance of using inclusive language has been promoted by feminists (and others involved in anti-oppressive practice). Although there is a sense that this achievement is vulnerable (and it has certainly been extensively trivialised and mocked) it has resulted in the development of language that is far more inclusive.

- There has been a recognition that societal developments and social policy initiatives effect men and women differently (because of their gender) and this has been challenged. The role of women as unpaid carers of (adult) family members with personal care needs is one example. Community care initiatives (social policy) have focused on enabling adults with personal care needs to stay at home. This has meant that there are pressures on women carers to carry on in their (unpaid) role.

  In children services the pressure on women is two fold. Firstly the societal pressure to be competent mothers and then the social pressure to move off benefits and return to work as soon as possible after having children.

The feminist perspective has promoted various responses. Firstly work with women is women centred. There is an explicit desire for the working relationship to empower the woman carer, parent or service user. As Dominelli (2002) has written "The assessment process is likely to involve redefining the problem being considered from a feminist perspective. This removes it from the private realm of a personal problem for which the woman is solely responsible and lodges it in the public domain as a social problem which she is experiencing individually along with a number of other women".

Secondly feminist social care and social work has promoted the need for women only space. This has implications for all services.

In mental health services the use of mixed wards has raised a range of concerns. At a fundamental level is the physical safety of women in-patients. The importance of single gender wards has been emphasised for some years.

Women only groups in mental health services and learning disability services are known to be empowering. Women only groups in leaving care services are also considered to enhance the self esteem and confidence of young women.

Thirdly the feminist perspective has called for social policy initiatives to provide equality of opportunity through the provision of adequate child care and, in adult services, a range of service options that will give carers a real choice.

Continuing Development

Although the feminist perspective has initiated some significant developments there are areas that it continues to grapple with. There are practical aspects and theoretical aspects.

In terms of practical considerations one of the feminist perspectives achievements is still not fully attained. The continuing level of domestic violence and the lack of a comprehensive, co-ordinated response that provides effective support for women and children and challenges violent men can leave women fearful about approaching professional agencies (Mullender 2002).

The feminist perspective has noticeably failed to adequately address structural inequalities within social care and social work organisations. In employment terms some 75% of the workforce in social care organisations are women. The proportion of men in senior management has remained stubbornly high and has only recently dropped below 75% of all senior managers.

In terms of continuing debates Orme (2002) has identified:-

1) The continuing uncertainty about whether women should be seen as different from men, as a special case. How far should feminist perspectives argue that women have qualities that are different to men? This could cut across arguments for equal opportunities and could result in reinforcing gendered roles (e.g.: women are better at caring than men).

2) The feminist perspective has criticised social care work for failing to recognise the power relationship and power imbalance between the woman professional and the woman service user. The woman professional is applying laws and policies that are discriminatory against women. Women need to influence the policy debates at National level as well as work at the level of the individual. This individual aspect includes acknowledging diversity and the power that exists in all relationships.

3) The way that feminist perspectives should seek to engage men has been contested. Some feminists would argue that this detracts from what should be the central focus, identifying the discrimination that women face and working with women to

counter this. Other feminists feel there needs to be engagement with men to address the levels of violence and inequality women experience from men and to call men to take responsibility for the way they develop their masculinity and to exercise the power they have in collaboration and dialogue with women.

The feminist perspective is an active illustration of the constructionist position. Society is socially constructed. If we want to, we can restructure society. However, the partial successes of the feminist movement also illustrate that the dominant power elites are quite satisfied with how society is structured. Whilst some ground has been conceded (or won by women), most of the land remains in the ownership of the same elite.

BLACK PERSPECTIVE

The black perspective has been developed by many different academics, practitioners and service users. There are a number of themes and elements some of which are located within a theoretical framework, whilst other elements are more applied.

Racism and White Ideology

The black perspective has made clear that racism is based on White European/White North American ideological beliefs about the claimed superiority of white people over non-white people.

This white ideology has been used to justify the enslavement of Africans from the early 17th Century onwards as well as the colonisation and control of Africa and other parts of the world from the 16th Century onwards.

At various times, the white ideology has invoked nature and God for its justification. It has also become self re-inforcing. British history and the manner in which Britain applied white ideology (slave trade and colonisation) leaves a residual white arrogance.

Other non white cultures have recognised differences but they have not developed the involved ideological claims of superiority. In this sense, racism is a white construction.

White Eurocentric Theory

It is against this backdrop of unconscious white views of superiority that all the significant psychological theories and social work theories have been developed.

White European culture has progressively championed the individual since the end of the Middle Ages. The rights of the individual and the importance of autonomy and self reliance have been key white themes since John Locke wrote in the late 1600s.

By contrast, many other cultures of the world have focused on the importance of achieving fulfillment by engagement and integration within a community. Mutuality, interdependence and spiritual connections are some of the goals that individuals within other cultures may strive for.

The inherent cultural biases within theories need to be recognised. Counselling approaches are deeply embedded in a white, Eurocentric, individualistic approach. Attachment theory has been used to validate the Eurocentric nuclear family and so implicitly denigrate alternative family structures and social arrangements relating to the care and nurture of children.

Within English social work, the practice of community social work has virtually died. English social work is focused on individual case management which, arguably, consists of little more than bureaucratic procedures.

Community social work is relevant for communities that face structural barriers and institutional discrimination. Black communities that experience economic and social disadvantage are more likely to benefit from community social work aimed at education, awareness raising and empowerment. However the triumph of individualistic social work case management disproportionately affects black communities compared to white communities (since poverty, unemployment, poor housing and poor educational opportunities disproportionately affect black people in Britain).

Feminist perspectives have been dominated by white women writers. In America, black women writers have formulated the concept of womanism. Womanism differs from feminism in that a woman comes to value herself as a woman in whatever role she may choose for herself. Within white feminism is the expectation that the woman will commit herself to meaningful action towards feminist goals. The womanist concept supports the development of a flexible, personal, positive self identity of what it means to be a woman (Ossana et al 1992).

More generally, many theories are based on an assumption of 'normality' as defined within White European or White North American culture. The more an individual, group or community from a non-white culture deviate from this 'normal' ideal, the increased likelihood that the individual or group will be pathologised (described negatively in terms of a disease or condition that is having a progressive effect). Arguably, it is within mental health services and children's services that this effect is most noticeable. The extent of institutional racism within mental health services has been a continuing problem (National Institute for Mental Health in England 2003). The exact reasons for the institutional racism are not clear. Factors such as aversive experiences in society (e.g.: racism) and structural inequalities also play a part. However, cultural views of what is 'normal' and therefore what is abnormal are likely to contribute.

In children services there is evidence of over representation of African children and dual heritage children in the looked after system. Also there is evidence that family centres are not equally accessible and black families do not get support that is available to white families (Dutt and Phillips 2000). Again, there are likely to be various factors that contribute to this of which an unconscious white racism towards black families is only one element.

<u>Development of Black Identity</u>

Within social care and social work there has been much debate about supporting positive identity formation. Often this debate has been held in children's services but it can equally apply to adult services.

One of the most influential theories of black identity formation is that of William Cross (1971, 1980 and 1991). The theory is termed Nigrescence, which means the process of becoming black in a white society. Cross identified that there are five stages that a black person will go through. These are:

1. Pre-encounter. The black person will identify with white people and white culture. The black person will be negative towards black people and could engage in self loathing.

2. Encounter. The person has an experience or a number of experiences that are unnerving. Examples include the person experiencing racism from white people. As a result of this, the person feels anxious and insecure. They start on a journey of questioning and self examination.

3. Immersion-Emmersion. The person 'immerses' themselves into black culture. They may change their style of dress, diet, friendships etc. There are aspects to the immersion stage that indicate the person lacks control, partly due to a reaction against their experience in the Encounter stage. However, the Emmersion process represents a process of regaining control, often by identifying with black role models.

4.   Internalisation. The person becomes secure in their black identity. This often results in a decline in the persons anti-white sentiment but a continuing sense of anger at racism. The person is usually able to mix socially with white people but their principle social network is with black people.

5.   Internalisation-commitment. The person has the ability to recognise the importance of countering all discrimination and is able to live out a concern for society as a whole. This stage is often associated with older adults.

Nigrescence theory could be useful for staff in children's services who are working with black adolescents. However, staff need to avoid using this (and any theory) in a blanket manner. This ties in with one of the themes of the black perspective – that there is diversity within black communities. A blanket application of any one anti-racist approach by services will be only partially effective.

Additionally some anti-racist practices are applied half heartedly. Owusu-Bempah (2002) is critical of racial identity and self concept programmes for black children who are looked after. Such programmes often focus on the individual child and ignore the broader structural reasons why the child entered the care system.

Elements of the Black Perspective

Any list of elements or aspects of the black perspective is going to be partial and incomplete. This is also because the development of the black perspective is one of the most dynamic debates in social work. Therefore what follows could easily become dated. The black perspective includes:

- A celebration of diversity. This includes recognising diversity between individuals, how families are structured, community relationships. Cultural diversity, language and history are to be enjoyed.
- Valuing the contribution of black people and the intellectual insights of black writers. Cross' theory of identity development is potentially relevant to all people who go through a process of personal liberation (women, gay men and gay women etc.).
- Recognition of the strengths of black people and communities. Many black voluntary organisations have started with little or no state support. There is an increasing range of services that seek

to support people from minority communities in culturally appropriate ways (e.g.: services for Asian women escaping domestic violence).

- Exposing the extensiveness of racism and highlighting the oppressive effects it has.
- Articulating the need for anti-racism practice to be dynamic and flexible, able to address the different forms that racism adopts (e.g.: institutional, unconscious etc.)
- Challenges White Eurocentric/White North American attitudes, beliefs, structures and systems.
- Is committed to equality and rights. Through the application of anti-racist practice other oppressive practices will be exposed and challenged.

Implications for Practice

Social work and social care staff need to be honest about the extensiveness and destructiveness of racism and the unconscious ways that white Eurocentric beliefs and practices are considered superior to non white beliefs and practices.

Staff need to avoid applying a blanket approach to their work with black people in which they prejudge the person and assume a certain text book, anti-racism strategy should be applied. Maybe that particular strategy is going to be beneficial but it should not be assumed.

Engage with the person and the broader community. Understand the person through their own words and their expression of their own identity.

Cultivate your own potential for learning and the development of your own anti-oppressive practice. Make clear you are open to being challenged.

SECTION TWO: ASSESSMENT

"Although assessment has been recognised as a core skill in social work and should underpin all social work interventions, there is no singular theory or understanding as to what the purpose of assessment is and what the process should entail."

(Social Care Institute for Excellence 2003: p5)

With no singular theory or approach to assessment, this section is potentially limitless. In order to clarify understanding, the section will look at assessment processes, concepts in assessment and models of assessment.

Reading this section, you will learn more about:

- Assessment as a process
- Models of assessment
- Needs led assessments
- Concepts of need
- Human Needs theories
- Bradshaw's taxonomy of need
- Acquired needs theory
- Outcomes focused assessment
- Strengths and resilience
- Risk assessment and risk management
- Defensible Decision making
- The Hindsight fallacy
- Risk compensation

FURTHER READING

This handbook provides an introduction to the main theories of social care. For further more detailed information on the areas covered in this section, see the following:

- Kemshall, H and Pritchard, J. (eds) (1996) *Good Practice in Risk Assessment and Risk Management.* (London) Jessica Kingsley.

- Milner, J and O'Byrne, P. (1998) *Assessment in Social Work.* (Basingstoke) MacMillan.

- Parker, J. and Bradley, G. (2003) *Social Work Practice: Assessment, Planning, Intervention and Review.* (Exeter) Learning Matters.

- Parsloe, P (ed) (1999) *Risk Assessment in Social Work and Social Care.* (London) Jessica Kingsley.

- Walker, S. and Beckett, C. (2003) *Social Work Assessment and Intervention.* (Lyme Regis) Russell House Publishing.

ASSESSMENT: PROCESS ISSUES

In terms of process, there are two main areas to consider:

- the assessment process
- assessment as part of a process

The Assessment Process

In considering the assessment process, Milner and O'Bryne present a five stage model of assessment (1998):

Stage 1: Preparation – which might include deciding who to see, what the purpose of the assessment is, what information will be needed etc.

Stage 2: Data collection – the worker gathers the necessary information.

Stage 3: Weighing up the data – the worker weighs up the information to reach an answer to the key question "is there a problem and is it serious?"

Stage 4: Analysing the data – the information is interpreted to gain a fuller understanding so that ideas for intervention can be developed.

Stage 5: Utilising the data – this stage is used to finalise judgements. The data will be used to evidence judgements and recommendations for intervention.

Assessment is presented as part of a wider overall process of social care in many texts. The process is generally seen in a similar way, as the start of the process, referred to by Taylor and Devine (1993) as the "basic helping cycle", illustrated in the following:

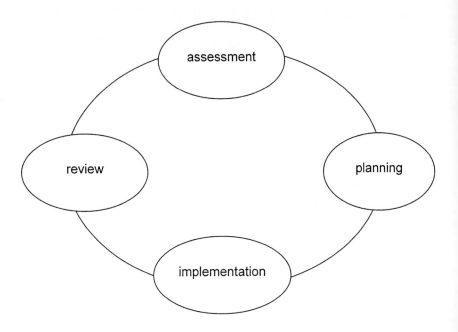

Others build on this idea by developing specific processes:

- The ASPIRE model (Sutton 1999)

AS	-	Assessment
P	-	Planning
I	-	Intervention
RE	-	Review and Evaluation

- The ASIRT model (Thompson 2005)

AS	-	Assessment – Which acts as the basis of an action plan which informs the:
I	-	Intervention – Assessment sets the objectives for the intervention.
R	-	Review – assessment becomes the baseline from which the review/evaluation operates.
T	-	Termination – Assessment objectives are considered in terminating intervention.

More recently however, some writers have started to dispute this, claiming that assessment can be a means to an end and doesn't necessarily lead to any intervention – such that the "cycle" is not always followed.

"While assessment is sometimes viewed as preceding intervention, increasingly assessment is being seen as a service in its own right rather than as a prelude to service delivery."

(SCIE 2003 page 2)

Theory and Assessment: The Links

Theory can be used in assessment in a variety of ways. To illustrate this, it is helpful to return to the 5 stage model of assessment proposed by Milner and O'Byrne (1998). See page 45.

Theory can be utilised at any of the stages and the practitioner's choice of theory could have a significant impact on the assessment and any subsequent plans, as follows:

Preparation. The practitioner's choice of theory is likely to impact on factors such as who they want to see, what type of information they deem necessary etc. So that for example, if a worker favours systems theory, they will probably plan to gather information not only from the service user but also from family members, other professionals etc.

Data Collection. The workers choice of theory can affect the questions they ask and the way they gather the information. For example, some practitioners always use the miracle question as part of their assessment process. Clearly where a worker adopts a biographical or narrative approach to their assessment this will effect the evidence that the worker gathers.

Weighing up and analysing the data. Here a practitioner will draw on a range of different theories – often more than one in any given assessment in order to make sense of all of the information they have gathered. If theory is not applied in some way at this point then the worker simply has a jumble of information which may or may not link together and which may or may not make sense.

Utilising the data. The way the information gathered in an assessment is utilised will depend on the theory or theories that the worker has applied in interpreting the data.

In science, a theory is viewed as helping to:

- Describe (e.g.: it answers the question "What is happening?")
- Explain (e.g.: it answers the question "Why is it happening?")
- Predict (e.g.: it answers the question "What is likely to happen next?")
- Control and/or bring about change (e.g.: "How can I change what may happen next?")

In many ways these four stages link to the stages of assessment as presented by Milner and O'Byrne which helps to clarify the way that theory and assessment are inextricably linked.

MODELS OF ASSESSMENT

In research published in 1993 Smale and Tuson (et al) identified three different models of assessment which are still seen as the three main models of assessment in social care services:

- The Questioning Model

   Here, the worker holds the expertise and follows a format of questions, listening to and processing the answers. The use of this model means that the assessment process largely reflects the worker's agenda.

- The Procedural Model

   Using this model, the worker gathers information to make a judgement about whether the service user fits the criteria for service provision. It is likely that a range of checklists will be used. The use of this model means that the assessment process largely reflects the agency agenda.

- The Exchange Model

   In this model, workers view people as experts on their own problems. The emphasis of this model is on exchanging information. The worker follows what people are saying rather than trying to interpret what they think is meant. The worker should help the service user to identify internal resources and potential. In this way the practitioner can consider how best to help service users mobilise their own resources in order to reach goals which are defined by the service user. The use of this model means that the assessment should reflect the service user's agenda.

   Smale et al make it clear that the exchange model is their preferred model. Working to this model however requires a great deal of skill. It means more than merely sharing assessments with service users. The model asserts that people in need and their family and friends will always know more about their problems and how they affect them, than workers. However, the model recognises that workers will have expertise in the process of problem solving. The aim of the worker should be to involve people in arriving at a compromise for meeting care needs. Rather than "making" an assessment the worker should manage the process.

Whilst making clear that they favour the exchange model, Smale et al acknowledge that workers can often feel pushed into the procedural model of assessment when they feel overwhelmed by eligibility criteria and the scarcity of resources. However, they point out that the exchange model can be useful in situations where resources are scarce as long term more stable solutions are likely to be reached and because inner resources can be maximised so that resource provision can be limited to very specific areas (if needed at all).

Smale et al accept that the questioning model is the most likely to be used when risk is the main emphasis of the assessment. Since specific answers to questions will be needed and to some extent the worker's agenda will need to be addressed.

CONCEPTS OF NEED

"Needs Led" Assessment

In recent years an emphasis has been put on needs led assessment. Many would argue that as the people carrying out assessment are often employed by agencies with limited resources that assessment can never be truly needs led.

There are further arguments that the concept of need in itself is not clear, so it is worth beginning with an overview of theories of need.

There are a number of theories of need. Probably the best known of which is Maslow's hierarchy of needs which is covered in Volume One. There are a range of other less well known relevant theories of need as follows:

Human Needs Theories

A number of writers have developed Maslow's ideas. One of the most well known is John Burton who has developed Maslow's hierarchy to apply it to theories about human conflict. Burton sees human needs not as a hierarchy but more as "an emergent collection of human development essentials. These needs do not have a hierarchical order. Rather, they are sought simultaneously in an intense and relentless manner." (Burton 1990).

Burton and other human needs theorists categorise needs in areas such as:

- Safety/security
- Belongingness/love
- Self esteem/personal fulfilment
- Identity
- Cultural security
- Freedom
- Justice
- Participation

Bradshaw's Taxonomy of Need

First developed by Jonathan Bradshaw in relation to the needs of older people, this was entitled a taxonomy of social need (see 1972). However, it is widely used in terms of health care.

Bradshaw refers to real need. He believes this to be a combination of four types of need:

- Normative need. This refers to needs which the expert/professional defines – these needs tend to be based on the professional's view of societal 'norms'.
- Perceived/felt needs. This refers to needs felt by the individual – in a way a self assessment. This type of need is sometimes referred to as a "want" rather than a need.
- Expressed need (demand). This refers to the needs expressed by people – this can be seen as felt need converted into expressed need when the person seeks assistance.
- Comparative need. This refers to the comparison that people make in defining needs – do we need what others have? etc. This is often referred to in understanding poverty – the concept of comparative poverty recognises that people may perceive themselves to be poor in comparison with others but this would not necessarily be viewed as "real" poverty.

Bradshaw claims that each of these areas of need overlaps and that it is perhaps somewhere in the overlap that "real need" can be found.

(Glendinning et al 2005)

Acquired Needs Theory

Proposed by McClelland (e.g.: 1961) this theory is also known as learned need theory or the three need theory. The idea is that we all have needs which fall into three general categories:

- Achievement (coded as N-Ach)
- Affiliation (coded as N-Aff)
- Power (coded as N-Pow)

McClelland proposed that a person's specific needs are acquired over time and are shaped by life experiences. He goes on to say that most people feel that one of these needs is more important than the others. As such he says which one of these is most important to us most affects our behaviour. Thus, he states that there are three types of people:

- Achievers
- Affiliation seekers
- Power seekers

This theory of need has been particularly influential in terms of understanding people at work and within organisations – as such it is covered in more detail in the management theory section of this book.

Outcomes Focussed Assessment

Perhaps the most recent approach to assessment is the outcome focussed approach. This has been developed by research carried out at the University of York. This approach is based on the social model of disability and empowerment (Harris et al 2005).

The approach identifies outcomes in three dimensions.

- outcomes involving change – for example improving self confidence, self-care skills or changes to accessibility of environments
- outcomes that maintain quality of life (or slow down deterioration in quality of life.) Sometimes referred to as maintenance outcomes.
- outcomes that are associated with the actual process of receiving services – such as feeling valued, being respected, feeling listened to etc.

Harris et al (2005) have developed an outcomes framework which categories outcomes into four areas – in many ways these four areas could be seen as needs. The three dimensions of outcomes could be applied to any of the four areas in the framework.

AUTONOMY OUTCOMES	PERSONAL COMFORT OUTCOMES
• Access to all areas of the home • Access to locality and wider environment • Communicative access • Financial security	• Personal hygiene • Safety/Security • Desired level of cleanliness of home • Emotional well-being • Physical health
ECONOMIC PARTICIPATION OUTCOMES	**SOCIAL PARTICIPATION OUTCOMES**
• Access to paid employment as desired • Access to training • Access to further/higher education/employment • Access to appropriate training for new skills (e.g.: lip reading)	• Access to mainstream leisure activities • Access to support in parenting role • Access to support for personal secure relationships • Access to advocacy/peer support • Citizenship

The outcomes focussed approach is seen as a user centred approach which involves the practitioner acting more as facilitator than assessor.

Research carried out by the Social Policy Research Unit (Harris et al 2005) identified that professionals find an outcome focussed approach to be an improvement on needs based assessment.

THE STRENGTHS PERSPECTIVE AND RESILIENCE

The strengths perspective is not a theory in itself. It has been developing for many years (arguably at least 40 years) with different writers contributing to its formation from their own fields.

The strengths perspective is partly a reaction against two features of social care/social work and health.

1. An increasing medical classification and diagnosis of individuals such that large sections of society could be labelled. This labelling is negative and has a deterministic theme (e.g.: you had a traumatic childhood therefore you will be a terrible parent and your children will end up in care) etc.

2. Assessments of needs have always been weighted towards listing peoples deficits, vulnerabilities and negative past experiences. In the current environment where demand for services is increasing but the resources available have barely increased, then there is an increased focus and heightening of service users lack of capability and risks.

In both of these key points, there is a structural or bureaucratic bias against recognising peoples strengths, abilities and resilience. Professionals, in serving the organisation more faithfully than they support the service user, make use of a language that is pathologising (the negative effects and degeneration that the person's condition is causing) and alienating.

Saleebey (1996) generated the following comparison of professional pathologising against the strengths perspective.

Pathology	Strengths
Person is defined as a 'case'; symptoms add up to a diagnosis.	Person is defined as unique; traits, talents, resources add up to strengths.
Therapy is problem focussed.	Therapy is possibility focussed.
Service user accounts are filtered by a professional to aid the generation of a diagnosis.	Personal accounts are the essential route to knowing and appreciating the person.
Professional is sceptical of personal stories and explanations.	Professional knows the person from the inside out.
Childhood trauma is the precursor or predictor of adult dysfunction.	Childhood trauma is not predictive; it may weaken or strengthen the individual.
Professional devises treatment or care plan.	Focus is aspirations of individual, family or community.
Professional is the expert of service user's life.	Individual, family or community are the experts.
Possibilities for choice, control, commitment and personal development are limited by label/diagnosis or condition.	Possibilities for choice, control, commitment and personal development are open.
Professionals knowledge, skills and connections are principle resources for service user.	The strength, capacities and adaptive skills of the individual, family or community are the principle resources.
Support is centred on reducing the effects of symptoms and the negative effects of emotions or relationships	Support is focussed on getting on with one's life, affirming and developing values and commitments and making or finding membership in a community.

The strengths perspectives argue that personal qualities and strengths can come out of and be formed by difficult life experiences. Resilience, independence, loyalty to one or more people can arise due to a painful or traumatic personal experience. People can develop great insight into their own situation.

An important source of strength can be cultural, community or personal stories or narratives. Cultural or community accounts of origins, development, migration and survival can provide inspiration and meaning (Saleebey, 1996).

Most professionals will probably say that they already apply the strengths perspective to that work. The counter to this is that many professionals only pay lip service to the strengths perspective. This is because the strengths perspective actually calls on the professional to move away from the objective, concrete and tangible.

The strengths perspective calls on the professional to connect with the individuals and families they work with in a manner that recognises hope, aspirations, spirituality, identity and belonging. The connection needs to be rooted in a true sense of equality.

The strengths perspective recognises that individuals and families have already been subjected to a range of demanding life events. Additionally, if people have had contact with health and social work services for some time they could have internalised the ideas of deficiency and needs. It is in addressing this that the professional's skills are called upon to work creatively with the service user and this can be very demanding. Individuals who have lived with grinding poverty or are on guard due to intimidatory and unpredictable racism are not going to automatically refer to the way they have benefited from their life experiences. The social worker and social care support worker are called to enable the service user to recognise the talents, resources, adaptive skills and support network the service user or family has.

The strengths perspective also recognises a brutal truth. Regardless of the input of professionals and paid support provided, if a family is to develop so that they don't need services, if an adult is to be largely independent in the community then it is due to their own abilities and strengths. Very few service users have a support worker at their shoulder 24/7.

Resilience Perspective

The resilience perspective is closely related to the strengths perspective. Sometimes resilience is seen as one aspect of the strengths perspective.

Resilience refers to supporting people develop their own reservoir of skills, abilities and knowledge. This personal reservoir includes the person's social support network. Ideally the individuals sense of the resources they have should be developed in depth (e.g.: strengthening existing family relationships or friendships) and across a broad range (the person is supported to try new experiences both so that they acquire new skills but also such that they meet new people).

The resilience perspective recognises that individuals can have difficulties in one area of their life. One of the ways a person overcomes a difficulty is by drawing on other aspects of their life either directly to problem solve, or indirectly such that the person has a sense that in other areas of their life they are doing well.

An example might be an older woman who cares for her husband who has dementia. The woman carer will be able to draw on her opportunities to meet with old friends, to meet her own adult sons, daughters and young grandchildren etc to sustain her in the caring role. The woman carer's daughter may give her advice on how to manage her caring role, but she may not. It could just be the enjoyment of being with grandchildren without having to actively worry for her husband that gives the woman carer the sense that she can return home to the caring task.

Most of us (but not all of us) respond positively to variety and stimulus in our life. Therefore the resilience perspective is as valid in children's services as it is in services for people with mental health problems, learning disabilities etc. Indeed there is a clear recognition that children are very resilient in most texts about safeguarding children.

Development of the Strengths Perspective

Each branch of social care and social work has developed its own literature on recognising people's strengths.

In mental health services, the recovery movement is closely related to aspects of the strengths perspective:

- The focus on wellness rather than illness
- The recognition of a person's individuality
- The de facto acknowledgement of the effects of the person's mental health problems but a recognition of the fact that this doesn't stop the person getting on with life

- Maintaining a sense of hope

In learning disability services, the strength's perspective (although not called that at the time) can be seen as far back as the 1960s.

- Jean Vanier has consistently talked about how much he learnt from people with learning disabilities he lived with, the strengths of people, the way his life has been enriched by living with people with learning disabilities (e.g.: Vanier 1988)
- Wolfensberger has been ambivalent towards professionals due to their failure to recognise the strengths of people with learning disabilities (e.g.: Wolfensberger 1988)
- Numerous other writers have championed the importance of engaging with people with learning disabilities as true equals and to recognise the way society benefits (e.g.: Brandon 1997, Neufeldt 1990, Williams 2006 etc).

In children's services the strengths and resilience of black families has been focussed on by various researchers who have been concerned by the way services have applied institutional racism in their work with black families:

- Owusu-Bempah and Howitt (1999) have discussed how black children can develop a positive sense of self in spite of racism and the importance of family relationships generally
- Hylton (1997) discusses survival strategies used by black families who experience racism including the importance of the whole (wider) family and spirituality
- Dutt and Phillips (2000) convey the importance of recognising the strengths of black families

These are just examples, but the strengths perspective has advocates in all areas of social care and social work.

Limitations and Critique of the Strengths Perspective

There is no acknowledgment of reluctant or resistant service users. Some service users don't want contact with services. Also some service users are not honest with social workers or social care staff. Due to this, many workers adopt a sceptical approach to what service users say. The worker may take the service users account seriously but they then test it, either through further questions or, more likely, by seeking independent confirmation from someone else. Such professional scepticism cuts across the strengths perspectives sense of values. In theory the worker needs to generate an environment where the service user or family member feels they can be honest. But if the service user or family member declares they have harmed a child or vulnerable adult, then the worker will have to initiate various actions.

The extent of illness or life trauma is minimalised. There is no intention to gloss over difficulties in a person's life. Cousins (1989) said that one should not deny the verdict (medical diagnosis, assessment etc) but should defy the sentence. A radical social perspective would question the societal move towards increased labelling. Rather than being defined by a label, it can be more productive to discuss with the person in what ways their hopes and aspirations are being restricted or limited. What are the practical impacts? What are the impacts on motivation, outlook and personal ambitions? Then move from there.

Application to Practice

The strengths perspective presents workers with both a challenge and an opportunity. To fully apply the strengths perspective, the worker must move away from bureaucratic, deficit led assessments. The worker needs to engage with the service user or family in the language of hope, aspirations and redemption (good things come out of painful experiences).

Ironically the opportunity is that in a time of increasingly restricted services, the worker who engages with an individual or family and supports them identify the strengths and abilities they have in themselves and their support network will leave the service user or family with something to build on.

RISK ASSESSMENT

Risk assessment is a key aspect of social care and social work practice. To understand the concept of risk assessment and the theoretical underpinning to this, it helps to understand that risk assessment is generally carried out in terms of two areas:

- The risks a person poses to others (dangerousness)
- The risks a person is subject to (vulnerability)

Whatever the focus of the assessment, the purpose is generally for the assessment to inform plans about intervention – generally referred to as risk management strategies.

The Risks a Person Poses to Others

In these situations risk assessment views risk as wholly negative and the focus is on accurately assessing the risks posed such that they can be avoided. Examples of this form of assessment are drawn from assessment of offending behaviour by workers in the criminal justice system or assessments by workers in mental health teams where a person is felt to pose a risk to others.

The Risks a Person is Subject to

Risk assessment in these situations doesn't necessarily focus on risk as wholly negative. There is a recognition that risk taking can be positive – e.g.: in increasing skills, developing confidence etc. Here the focus is on identifying risks, identifying which risks are acceptable and which are not acceptable.

The assessment should lead to strategies for risk management which focus on balancing the benefits of risk taking with any potential harm.

Interestingly, it can be argued that risk assessment in terms of child protection and, to an increasing extent, adult protection combine aspects of dangerousness and vulnerability assessments. So that for example a risk assessment may explore the "vulnerability" of the child and the "dangerousness" of the care giver.

Two basic techniques are used in risk assessments:

- Actuarial Assessment

- Clinical Assessment

Actuarial Assessment

This is developed from insurance industry methods for risk calculation. It is basically about a statistical calculation of risk. The focus is on probabilities which are generally expressed in numerical terms – usually percentages.

Actuarial assessment is seen as more accurate than clinical assessment but there are always problems with statistical measures. The approach is reliant on research findings about groups and it can be difficult to transfer learning from generalised information to individual situations. Therefore the more infrequent the risk, the less accurate the actuarial prediction will be.

Actuarial assessment is limited in terms of risk management solutions in that this type of assessment provides a prediction about likelihood rather than offering any understanding about the risks, possible effects etc.

Clinical Assessment

Clinical assessment is a much more individual assessment method. It is undertaken by workers on a case by case basis. Clinical assessment is based on a professional judgement of risk and as such can be value based and subjective. Clinical risk assessment has a poor record of accuracy.

It is largely accepted that there are two forms of error with clinical assessment – false negatives and false positives (see later).

Despite the unreliability of clinical assessment, it does have some strengths, in that this individualised form of assessment can offer more than simple probability predictions. This type of assessment can provide an analysis which offers an understanding of the nature of risk and ideas for risk management strategies.

Holistic Risk Assessment

Recognising that neither of these two approaches are wholly effective, writers now promote an approach which combines the positives of each method (e.g.: Limandri and Sheridan, 1995,

Kemshall, 2002). This holistic approach combines probability predictions and ideas about the nature of the risk. These combined methods are often referred to as "second generation" assessment tools (Monahan and Steadman 1994). Kemshall sees the holistic approach to risk assessment as essential to individual case work. She sees this approach as highlighting areas for significant intervention and change as part of the care management process (Kemshall 2002).

Conclusions and Decisions in Risk Assessment

No risk assessment process can be totally accurate. As previously stated both actuarial approaches and clinical approaches are not "fail safe".

It is generally accepted that there are two types of inaccuracies – false positives and false negatives. The following table taken from Walker and Beckett (2005: p86) clarifies this.

True and false positives and negatives

True positives	Situations identified as high risk where the harmful event actually occurs in the absence of protective intervention.
False positives	Situations identified as high risk where the harmful event actually would not occur even in the absence of protective intervention.
True negatives	Situations identified as low risk where no harmful event occurs.
False negatives	Situations identified as low risk, but where the harmful event does nevertheless occur.

This table is helpful in that it illustrates how, when carrying out a risk assessment and planning intervention, a worker can "go wrong" in two ways. For example, let's take a situation where a child is removed from her parents care because a risk assessment has concluded that she is at risk of significant harm. Using the concept of true and false negatives and positives there are 2 potential outcomes:

True Positive   -   If the child would have remained in her parents care, she would have been harmed ie: the assessment and intervention was "right".

False Positive   -   If the child had remained at home, she would not have come to any harm ie: the assessment and intervention was "wrong". In actual fact, since the removal of the child will in itself cause distress and 'harm' to the child further harm has been caused.

In another situation a child is left in the care of his parents because a risk assessment has concluded that there is a low risk of harm. Again there are 2 potential outcomes:

True negative   -   The child remains at home and comes to no harm ie: the risk assessment was "right".

False negative   -   The child remains at home and is harmed ie: the assessment was "wrong".

Understanding the concept of true and false positives and negatives helps to illustrate the double bind that social work and social care staff often find themselves in. "Damned if you do, damned if you don't." This has led to various discussions about decision making. As a result of which Carson (1996) introduced the concept of defensible decision making.

Defensible Decision Making

In recognition of the fact that risk assessment is a highly fallible process, with no guarantee of certainty, Carson argues that the key skill is to arrive at decisions in a manner that a reasonable body of co-professionals would also have followed. This makes the decision defensible if brought to account.

Aspects that make up a defensible decision include:

- all reasonable steps are taken
- reliable assessment methods have been used
- information is collected and thoroughly evaluated
- decisions are recorded
- staff work within agency policies and procedures
- staff communicate with others and seek information they do not have

The Hindsight Fallacy

Introduced by Macdonald and Macdonald (1999) this concept is in common language ("in hindsight....." "with the benefit of hindsight....." etc). When a negative result occurs – for example a risk assessment has concluded a low risk and then a child is harmed, the assumption is that a serious mistake has been made. However, this is not always the case. The risk assessment may have led to a highly "defensible decision".

"....a bad outcome in and of itself does not constitute evidence that the decision was mistaken. The hindsight fallacy is to assume that it does."

Walker and Beckett (2005) conclude that it is vital when reviewing outcomes to recognise situations where there were risk indicators that should have been noted (a mistake was made) and situations where the significance "could not have reasonably been seen without the benefit of hindsight." (2005: p.87).

Approaches to Risk/Intervention Strategies

Having considered the main approaches to risk assessment and the potential outcomes of risk assessment, we can move on to look at some of the main intervention approaches. The main intervention approaches can be categorised into:

- risk elimination
- risk reduction
- risk minimisation
- risk management

Risk Elimination
Risk elimination refers to an approach which seeks to completely eliminate risks. This is a practically impossible aim in social work and social care. There are however a few examples where a risk is entirely influenced by one environmental factor, where this environmental factor can be changed.

Risk Reduction
This approach seeks to "reduce" the risks or the likelihood of identified risks occurring.

Risk Minimisation
This approach is most often referred to as harm minimisation. Essentially this approach is about minimising the impact of the risk.

Risk Management
Risk management approaches seek to "manage" risks rather than attempting to eliminate them. Risk management strategies are usually devised on a case by case basis using aspects of risk reduction and harm minimisation.

Risk Compensation

It is widely accepted that people adapt their behaviour based on their perceptions of risk. Such that, for example, where people feel that they face significant risk, they will ensure that they employ safety conscious behaviours. Where people feel "safe" in the knowledge that risks are minimised, their behaviour will adapt to their perception of risk such that they may place themselves at heightened risk. People are in essence lulled into a false sense of security. This is widely demonstrated in research relating to road safety – for example, cyclists wearing helmets will take more risks because they feel "safe" wearing helmets.

In devising risk management strategies, it is important to address potential behaviour changes created by risk compensation. As a straightforward example – many social care organisations have made a conscious decision not to provide self defence training for staff because of fear that staff will adapt their behaviour and place themselves in more risky situations. They may stay and "fight" rather than seek to leave when faced with an incidence of violence and aggression. When in fact leaving is always the safest and most preferable option. Keeping safe is more about being equipped with knowledge and information about risk and being able to identify risk than knowing what to do in terms of self defence.

Understanding the concept of risk compensation is important in terms of discussing risk management strategies with service users. How will they ensure they contribute to the strategy through their behaviour etc?

SECTION THREE: COUNSELLING

Counselling theory is a very broad term. In outline, it is commonly seen as the development of a relationship between a counsellor or therapist and an individual who wants an opportunity to explore their life. (Sometimes the relationship is between a counsellor and a couple or a family). In counselling theory, the type and quality of the relationship is a key element in the therapeutic process. The aim of the relationship is to free the individual so that they can live their life as they want to. As such, an understanding of counselling theory can assist any social care worker.

Reading this section, you will learn more about:

- Person centred counselling
- Existential counselling
- Rational Emotive Behaviour Therapy
- Cognitive Behavioural Therapy (CBT)
- Brief Solution Focused Therapy (BSFT)
- Psychodynamic approaches
- Transactional Analysis (TA)
- Conflict resolution
- The narrative approach

FURTHER READING

This handbook provides an introduction to the main theories of social care. For further more detailed information on the areas covered in this section, see the following:

- Craig, Y. (ed) (1998) *Advocacy, Counselling and Mediation in Casework: Processes of Empowerment.* (London) Jessica Kingsley.

- Dallos, R. and Draper, R. (2000) *An Introduction to Family Therapy.* (Buckingham) OU Press.

- Dryden, W. (2006) *Counselling in a Nutshell.* (London) SAGE.

- Feltham, C. and Horton, I. (2005) *The Sage Handbook of Counselling and Psychotherapy.* (London) SAGE.

- Mearns, D. and Thorne, N. (1999) *Person Centred Counselling in Action.* Second Edition. (London) SAGE.

- Miller, L. (2005) *Counselling Skills for Social Work.* (London) SAGE.

- Milner, J. and O'Byrne, P. (2002) *Brief Counselling: Narratives and Solutions.* (Basingstoke) Palgrave MacMillan.

- O'Connell, W. (1998) *Solution Focused Therapy* (London) SAGE.

- Sedan, J. (2005) *Counselling Skills in Social Work Practice.* (Buckingham) OU Press.

COUNSELLING THEORY

It is more accurate to use the plural term 'theories'. There are lots of different approaches. Examples include:

- Person centred counselling (strongly influenced by Carl Rogers)
- Existential counselling
- Rational Emotive Behaviour Therapy
- Cognitive Behavioural Therapy (commonly referred to as CBT)

The common element in these approaches is that the individual meets with a professional and that relationship enables the individual to address problems or questions.

Each counselling theory has their own view of humanity and why people experience problems. Each theory then goes on to explain how these problems can be addressed.

Person Centred Counselling

The person centred approach views the individual as the expert on their own life. Each person is fully capable of fulfilling their own potential. All a person needs to achieve their life goals is a sense of acceptance and positive regard. Unfortunately in life, positive regard is made conditional on the person living a certain way.

If an individual feels that they must live a certain way to receive conditional positive regard and these expectations are not a true expression of their individuality, then psychological disturbance occurs. The psychological disturbance will continue for as long as the person feels they have to live in that way.

Person centred counselling argues that to address this, the individual needs to enter into a therapeutic relationship which consists of three key qualities:

1. Unconditional positive regard. The counsellor accepts the person unconditionally. The person is free to express all thoughts and feelings without risk of rejection or condemnation. The person does not have to 'earn' the counsellor's positive regard.

2. Empathic understanding. The counsellor seeks to accurately understand the person's thoughts and feelings. By perceiving the world from the person's own perspective, the counsellor demonstrates that the person's view has value and they are accepted. One of the techniques used in empathic understanding is reflective questioning. The counsellor listens to the person and to ensure they have understood them, paraphrases what the person has just said, often in the form of a question.

3. Congruence. The counsellor must be authentic and genuine. The counsellor has to be transparent, there is no hidden agenda.

If these conditions are met, then person centred counselling claims that therapeutic change will occur. In fact, if these conditions are met in relationships the person has with other people (friends, family etc) then these relationships will be as therapeutic as a relationship with a counsellor.

The counsellor's role is to enable the person to encounter and engage with themselves and become more aware of their own thoughts, feelings and emotions.

Existential Counselling

Simply put, existential counselling is about why we exist. What are our ideals, priorities and values? Once we identify these we should seek to achieve them. Existential counselling recognises that our priorities and values can change and this affects our identity. Additionally, we find ourselves living under the expectations and demands of other people's priorities and values. A well adjusted response is to recognise the complexities in our life but maintain our own priorities. However, at one time or another, many or most of us compromise ourselves and live according to other peoples priorities or values.

The counsellor's role in existential counselling is to enable the person to understand their values and ideals.

Existential theory has developed a four part framework (which the counsellor may use as a prompt). The four parts are:

1. The physical dimension of health, body and the natural world.

2. The psychological or personal dimension which includes intimate relationships with others and engaging with ourselves.

3. The social dimension of public relationships

4. The spiritual dimension of ideals, personal philosophy and meaning.

The counsellor will seek to support the person engage with themselves in all four of these dimensions.

Rational Emotive Behaviour Therapy

Rational Emotive Behaviour Therapy (REBT) recognises that we have emotions but views strong emotional reactions as leading to mental health problems. REBT argues that strong emotional reactions are often a result of a person believing that something 'must', 'should' or 'ought' to happen. For example in response to a relationship ending a person may say "I can't go on." REBT argues that the rational response is to recognise that there may be difficulties but the person can still function.

REBT claims that people are burdened with a sense of 'musts' and 'shoulds'. However, we have a choice and individuals can select alternative attitudes that are more rational.

The counsellors role in REBT is far more directive and can include disputing the person's view of their irrational beliefs. The aim is for the person to recognise that their irrational beliefs caused their problems (and not the initial trigger events, such as redundancy, or acquiring a disability etc). The person must develop rational alternatives so that their emotional and behavioural response still enables them to function.

Cognitive Behavioural Therapy

Cognitive Behavioural Therapy (CBT) or counselling is a direct application of cognitive-behavioural theory.

In cognitive behavioural theory there is the realisation that our thoughts (cognitions) can have a very positive effect on our behaviours. Cognitive behavioural theory recognises that we have the capacity to do something that we may not like (in the short term) if we believe it will result in benefits in the medium to long term. A basic example is the person who goes to university for three years (so is poor, loaded with assignments and could get thrown off the course for not doing course work) in the belief that they will get a well paid job that they otherwise may not have got.

Cognitive behavioural theory also recognises that our thoughts can result in holding us back, even when, objectively speaking, there is no reason to think this.

A simple example could be as follows:

A teenage young woman who is in a dance competition comes in fourth place. The teenager could think "If I practice hard and get more coaching, I can improve and get a better placing next time." Or the young woman could think, "The others were better than me, I'm not going to do this again, coming fourth is as good as being laughed at."

We can, at times, all have negative thoughts (It's not worth it! etc.). When a person has so many negative thoughts that it starts to effect their ability to engage with others, then it may be that cognitive behavioural therapy (or counselling) could help.

The aim of the therapy (or counselling) is to support the person understand their own thoughts and then to test them against events in the service users own world. Often there may be some form of 'homework' where the service user has to apply a new attitude or approach to one area of their life.

Cognitive behaviour therapy requires a high level of co-operation between service user and therapists. The usefulness of CBT has been highlighted in working with individuals who have depression, anxiety disorders, obsessive compulsive disorders, psychosis and Schizophrenia (e.g.: Bradshaw 2003 and Messari and Hallam 2003). The therapy or counselling may need to be relatively long term (over a year) but some service users report a clear sense of improvement in their condition.

Perspectives on Counselling

Counselling and 'talking treatments' have become so important that most Department of Health documents on mental health look to the availability of counselling as one of the key means to enhance well being in the population.

Although there is increasing research evidence about the benefits of counselling, it is not clear why or what makes it beneficial. Arguably, it may simply be the opportunity to discuss our own hopes and problems for an hour a week with a person who is friendly and accepting.

Counselling should not be seen as a blanket 'cure' and there are people who will find that counselling has not been helpful.

Counselling may not be that useful for some people. Possible examples include:

- individuals who are not articulate or who have communication difficulties
- people whose values are based around family and community (counselling is seen as emphasising the individual)
- people who don't want to go to counselling

Counselling and Social Care

The main learning points for care staff to be aware of in respect of counselling are:

- Counselling could well be beneficial for a person you are supporting. Counselling is becoming more accessible through G.P. surgeries and mental health teams. Additionally, there are voluntary counselling services and counsellors who work privately.
- It is not for care staff to be a counsellor but some of the attitudes and skills promoted by counselling theory could be effectively used by care staff. For example:

    - recognise that individuals are experts of their own situation
    - acknowledge that all people have the potential for personal growth
    - service users should be listened to by staff. If staff use empathic listening and reflective questions, they should be able to understand what the service user is seeking to convey. Additionally, it is best if the staff member is congruent and genuine.
    - Staff should adopt an approach of unconditional positive regard.

- There are different ways that an event in a person's life can be viewed. Staff may be able to suggest to a service user a way of viewing a situation that is realistic but positive.

BRIEF SOLUTION FOCUSED THERAPY

Brief Solution Focused Therapy is attributed to the work of Steve De Shazer (1985) and his colleagues at the Brief Family Therapy Centre in the United States. During the early 1980s De Shazer and his colleagues considered that service users who were attending therapy needed to focus on what they wanted to achieve through therapeutic support rather than the problem that led them to seek help in the first place.

Brief Solution Focused Therapy (BSFT) has several key elements. These include:

- The belief that people who come to sessions due to past difficulties are able to develop strategies to address their difficulties or problems within the counselling relationship.
- The counsellor/practitioner does not focus on the past. There is more emphasis placed on the present and future
- The service user – counsellor relationship is goal orientated. These goals are:

    - generated by the service user
    - small rather than large
    - described in specific, concrete and behavioural terms
    - relate to interactional and interpersonal rather than individual terms
    - realistic and achievable

- The counsellor's skills lie in asking questions that draw out the service users strengths and skills and enables the service user to see how they can use their own skills to achieve their goals

Duration and Outline of BSFT

The number of sessions can range between 1 and 12. The average number of sessions appears to be about 5. Sessions are usually held in a 3 or 4 month period. However, a service user could return after this period if they felt it necessary.

Typical themes in BSFT sessions include:

- the outcomes (goals) that the service user wants to achieve

- the strengths and resources of the service user, including their social network
- identifying exceptions. This is identifying an occasion when all the triggers were present that could have caused the problem but the service user was able to deal with it themselves and prevent the problem occuring
- discussing changes in the service users life from session to session and noting successes
- confirming what the strategies are that the service user finds helpful in achieving the changes

The Counsellor/Practitioners' Use of Questions

As already mentioned, one of the skills of the counsellor/practitioner is the use of supportive questions aimed at enabling the service user to recognise their own strengths and abilities.

Various types of questions are used. These include:

- The Miracle Question. This supports the service user identify how the future will be different when the problem is no longer present. The practitioner should shape the miracle question to be relevant to the person they are with. One aspect that could be focused on is how the service user would know or sense that the miracle (the problem they had in the past has now gone) had occurred.
- Scaling questions. The service user is asked to score the present on a scale of 1 to 10. The practitioner could then ask what would it take to move one point up the scale. This can also be used for identifying immediate goals.
- Exception finding questions. The practitioner supports the service user identify the successful strategies they have used in the past. The intention is to give the service user the confidence to apply their own strategies to improve their situation.
- Coping questions. These seek to support the service user recognise the general strengths and resources they have. This approach aims to assist the service user move from an internalised problem focussed narrative to recognition of their capabilities.

BSFT has become an increasingly popular tool in social care practice. The underlying principal of this approach is that people can get preoccupied with their problems and are not able to see past them with any confidence. Workers use this approach to support service users to see past the difficulties and reframe the individual's way of looking at them; this in turn promotes a change in the way the problems are viewed and the solutions are utilised.

PSYCHODYNAMIC APPROACHES

Psychodynamic theory was commonly drawn on by social workers in the 1960s and 70s. Since then its use in social work has progressively declined. It is now only really used by psychologists and a small minority of social workers. Psychodynamic theory is discussed here since some of its insights can be relevant to understanding the situation of service users.

<u>Origins</u>

Sigmund Freud's early development of psychodynamic theory has been developed by a number of writers. Freud claimed that we have various levels of conscious and unconscious thought. There is the Id which is the source of basic urges and the drive to survive (hence its association with sexuality). The superego is the conscious, 'public' expression that seeks to convey that we are doing what is socially acceptable. The ego was the part of the unconscious that tries to mediate between these two. The relationship between the unconscious and the conscious is a dynamic, active one. But the individual may not be (and often isn't) aware of the interactions that are occurring within themselves and engages in behaviours that are expressions of their deep unconsciousness and then seeks to rationalise them through the ego and superego.

One of the claims of psychodynamic theory is that early, negative experiences that are painful for the child are buried deep in their unconscious. However, these experiences are not lost and shape the person's relationships with the people they come into contact with from then on (although the individual may not realise what they are doing and why).

Bion (1962) has developed this idea especially in terms of the main care giver and the young child. Various terms have been developed to explain the processes that occur between the young child and the primary care giver. There is not the scope here to cover them. However, Bion (1962) and other writers reinforce the view that the quality of relationships from early infancy onwards will shape the child's developing personality and character. If the care givers actions (or inaction) are not adequate this will have a negative impact on the child's emotional development and their ability to engage in relationships.

One of the early themes of psychodynamic theory is that we dislike the emotional state of anxiety but are beset with it. Therefore we develop various defence mechanisms to protect ourselves from anxiety.

These defences include:

- Denial (claiming or acting as if an event or experience hasn't happened)
- Repression (memories of a bad experience are banished, present desires are suppressed e.g.: sexual desire for a person)
- Projection (claiming someone has an emotional state that the first person actually has, e.g.: the unfaithful man questioning his partner because he claims the partner is planning to be unfaithful)
- Displacement (if a person is angry with their partner, they shout at their children instead)

Freud also articulated the experience of transference. This refers to a process that occurs between the service user and the professional who is actively working with the service user. The service user transfers onto the professional emotions that have been generated as a result of past relationships. These emotions can relate to actual events in the person's past relationship or imagined (desired) event. The professional needs to be aware of the possibility of transference so they can work with it if it happens.

Psychodynamic theory argues that to understand why we do things and have the type of relationships we have, we need to look at our present emotions and actions and unpick why we are doing what we are doing. We need to understand and articulate the course or origins of our emotions and anxieties. Only by doing this can we start to consciously control our behaviour.

The counsellor or therapist has to coach, support, encourage, question assumptions, challenge etc to enable the service user to develop insight. Some therapists still use dream interpretation as a 'gateway' into the unconscious.

Implications for Social Work

Psychodynamic intervention requires long term commitment on the part of the counsellor/therapist and the service user. In modern social work most social workers cannot provide this. Clearly the social worker could recommend a psychodynamic approach if they felt the service user would benefit.

The psychodynamic approach also cautions the social worker or support worker that with some service users behavioural approaches will not work. An individual may need to do something (parent a child in a certain way, relate to their partner respectfully etc) and despite all the accepted behavioural learning techniques (role modelling, rehearsal, praise) the service user keeps relapsing. The psychodynamic response may be to say that this could be an example where the person has had very negative past experiences that are now deep in their unconscious. The person is unaware of how these unconscious fears continue to shape their behaviour today. The only way for the person to control their behaviour is to address their unconscious fears and anxieties.

There is possibly another reason why social workers may also have moved away from psychodynamic theory. It is now clear that Freud realised what was happening when young women came to him telling him of sexual encounters with their fathers. The young women were being sexually abused and raped. Freud buried this (a more sympathetic reading is that Freud was never fully sure what was happening). Instead Freud talked of children having sexual fantasies towards their parents. Arguably, this put back the protection of children from sexual abuse by 60 years. Since one aspects of Freud's early writing is wrong, it does not mean all psychodynamic theory should be rejected. But within social work there appears to be an unconscious rejection of psychodynamic theory partly because of this.

TRANSACTIONAL ANALYSIS

Transactional analysis is a framework for understanding (analysing) the communication between people (transactions). As such this theory can help explore relationships. The idea was first developed by Harris (1970) and has since been further developed by various writers (e.g.: Berne 1978, Jacobs 1999 etc).

Transactional analysis (TA) is based on an understanding of ego states and personality development. The idea is that we all have certain elements to our personality:

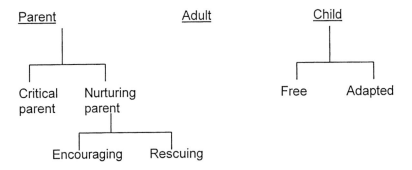

When we communicate with others, we may be "in" different states to the other person, which will impact on relationship development.

It is more straightforward to understand this using diagrammatic representation, as follows:

Appropriate Relationships

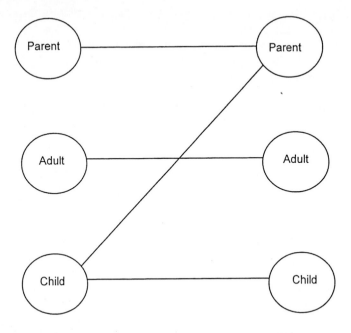

Generally complimentary relationships are evenly balanced
(represented by the straight lines). So that a parent to parent, adult to
adult, child to child relationship is appropriate. A parent to child
interaction is also appropriate and this may in fact appropriately
denote the transactions between two adults. For example, where one
person is acting in a sulky, childish manner, it might be appropriate for
the other to respond in a parental way.

Problematic Relationships

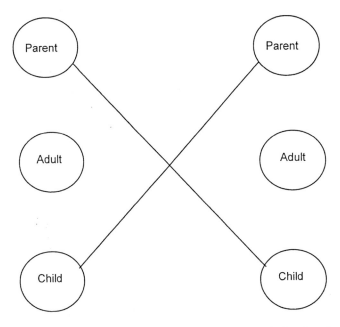

Sometimes people may experience difficulties in relating to others, which can be as a result of their childhood, their personality or the situation they find themselves in. For example, a service user may feel powerless because of the power invested in the social care worker – this may lead them to respond to the worker in a child to parent manner. The worker is likely to want to engage with the service user on an adult to adult basis – so there are likely to be problems in the interactions and relationship.

Berne (1978) suggests that life experiences can "hook" our parent and our child which can then take over from our adult (which as adults is the preferred state). He suggests that professionals may be able to support service users to rehearse using their adult state in communications more often – in this way practitioners may be able to support service users in developing their dysfunctional relationships.

Application to Practice

Transactional analysis is a complex theory based within the psychodynamic approach. In relation to Freud, the "parent" part of personality is viewed as the superego, the "adult" as the ego and the "child" as the id. What is presented here is a simplified explanation of the approach. Social care staff and social workers should not attempt to use their basic understanding in a therapeutic manner. However, having a basic understanding of TA can help staff to recognise why people respond to them in certain ways and why they may respond to others in different ways etc. It can also help to explain why relationships may become problematic and dysfunctional.

CONFLICT RESOLUTION

Conflict resolution is a model or approach rather than a theory. It is a very applied model which makes clear the skills, values and attitudes that are needed to enable conflict resolution to be achieved.

Conflict resolution has been characterised by the initial headline of "win/win". However, there is significantly more to it than just saying that phrase as a mantra.

Stages, Skills and Attitudes

Conflict resolution is characterised by a number of stages. Different writers have generated different numbers of stages. The general process is as follows:

1. When you are in a situation of potential conflict with another person, you need to avoid entering into an adversarial and defensive approach. The initial task is to have an attitude where you want yourself and the person who is in dispute with you, to benefit from any shared decision (win/win).

    To do this, the starting point is to find out what the needs are of each party. Skills required include supportive questioning (to identify the other person's needs), listening and the ability to communicate your own needs. In communicating your own needs you should be assertive, use the 'I' word without expectations of what the other person should do. Conflict resolution recognises that the person could be very angry with you. Options include:

    -   Don't defend yourself at first, this will antagonise the situation
    -   Deal with their emotions; explicitly acknowledge that you recognise how angry they are
    -   Acknowledge their perspective. You do not need to agree with them but you do need to understand them

    This process should enable the person to calm down. From then on the process should follow the same stage process.

    One of the key elements to conflict resolution is attitude:

- there must be an openness to recognise the benefit of differences
- a willingness to adapt or trade for mutual benefit
- a view that the difficulty is to be addressed and not the person
- disagreements or potential conflicts are not a problem. They are an opportunity to engage with the other person.

2. Once the needs of each individual have been expressed, the next stage is negotiation. As part of this, the focus must remain on the issue. Where possible, explicitly acknowledge common ground. If it appears to be a big problem, can it be broken down?

If negotiations get heated:

- manage your own emotions
- let some barbed comments go without responding to them
- have a break but agree when to resume

In seeking a solution:

- make a trial proposal
- suggest a trade "I will do this if you do that"
- make an agreement time limited or temporary

3. Mediation

If it is not possible to reach a win/win situation, it may be necessary to go for mediation.

A mediator requires various skills, including:

- being explicit that mutual benefit is the aim
- the mediator must have a clear sense that both parties are willing to address the problem
- enabling each party to express themselves and check the other party has understood them
- an ability to encourage suggestions (the mediator should avoid making their own suggestions)
- discourage personal comments or behaviours that could be provocative (name calling; ignoring; threats; belittlement etc)

4.   Resolution

Be clear about the agreement. It is easy for two people to leave a conflict situation with each of the people having a different understanding of what has been agreed.

Application to Practice

Conflict resolution and mediation are models rather than theory. Many of the skills required in conflict resolution are closely related to counselling skills (supportive questioning, reflecting back comments to ensure there is understanding and agreement etc.). Social care workers are often in situations of conflict and an understanding of processes of conflict resolution and mediation is therefore important.

NARRATIVE APPROACH

Like many theories and models discussed in this book, the narrative approach is born from a number of birth parents. Its use in the UK is in danger of being reduced to the practice of a small number of social workers who are not in mainstream services or who defy mainstream services.

In this section we will give a brief overview of the narrative approach and then describe some of its uses in social care and social work.

Overview

The narrative approach is in many ways self explanatory. It is where the social worker or social care worker gives the service user the opportunity to describe their own life in their own words.

It is one of the key ways that the worker can truly get to know the service user. The narrative approach is valued since it enables the service user to describe their own identity in the form they wish to. It also provides the service user with the opportunity to re-affirm or to redefine their identity.

The narrative approach is also useful since it enables the person to describe themselves in a manner that includes inconsistencies, contradictions, missed opportunities, regrets, uncertainty etc.

Potentially the narrative approach can be used in individual work as well as group work. Even in individual work, it is a time consuming approach and in groupwork it absorbs far more time (since over the life of the group, all members will need the opportunity to contribute).

Partly due to the time issue, it is often only utilised by workers who can devote the necessary time.

1.   One of the main applications of the narrative approach is in promoting anti-discriminatory practice. The opportunity for the person to self define their identity has been seen as a vital aspect of empowerment in work with Black and Asian service users. The narrative approach is also viewed as enabling service users to understand some of the pressures they have faced and the impact that discriminatory experiences have had on them. Through the supportive questions of a member of

staff, the service user should learn to realise that the oppressive features in their life were external to themselves. The worker's role is to enable the service user to reframe their life experiences, possibly by deconstructing some of the person's life events. It can be helpful for the worker to say to the service user they are going to deconstruct or reframe some of their life experiences. However, it is not unusual for service users to be very aware of the nature of the discrimination and inequality they have experienced. Often one of the key aspects is having a professional affirm the unfairness; to validate the service user's sense of oppression.

The narrative approach has also been used in feminist social work (e.g.: Reissman, 2000) and in work with adults with mental health problems (e.g.: Ridgeway, 2001).

2.   It is not unusual for service users to adopt a narrative approach in their ordinary contact with social care workers or social workers.

Social care professionals can sometimes resent the time that service users take to answer a question. The social care professional can label the service users discussion as 'rambling' or 'off the point'.

In many ways the service user is (probably unconsciously) engaging in an act of resistance against social care and social work practices that seek to reduce service users to manageable time slots or processable assessment forms.

Many social care practices can appear to be a mass production of personal care tasks. The community support workers who only have 15 or 30 minutes with a service user may ask the service user a question and find the service user gives an answer that is longer than one sentence and has the support worker resenting the time spent listening to the service user.

The assessor visits the service user with their assessment form and wants an answer that neatly fits into the boxes they have on their form. The assessor may not want to address some of the boxes at all. But peoples lives are not compartmentalised. Something has happened in the service user's life that was triggered by something else that arose because of contact with a person who ....

The service user who gives long answers is (unconsciously) conveying that their lives have breadth (multi layered or complex) and have a depth (time). When they reduce their experiences to one or two sentences, it strips them of their personality and identity.

When the service user does take time to talk round a question from a worker, does the worker start looking at their own watch?

When a person goes through a period of change (and usually a professional is involved because the service user has found the changes very demanding on their personal resources, they are stretched to the limit) it is not unusual for the person to need time to absorb what some of the consequences are for them now in the light of their previous (recent) lifestyle.

Some people require the time to talk round a subject or personal experience to absorb it. In this respect, the narrative approach can be helpful to enable the person to psychologically and mentally adjust to their new situation.

3. Whilst this third point is relatively minor, aspects of the narrative approach can be useful for mutual respect in a team. If there is the opportunity, team members can be given the chance to describe themselves in terms of their own identity and values. When we start working with someone, we can jump to an assumption that they would define themselves as Black or as English etc (based on their appearance). However, if each team member is invited to describe themselves in their own words, then it can result in a greater sense of mutual respect and facilitate communication as team members can feel more at ease with each other.

Application to Practice

Potentially, the narrative approach still has a lot to offer social care and social work. Unfortunately, it is not used a great deal partly because it does not sit easily with the social care requirements for 'mass production' of social care or social work requirements to complete neat assessment forms.

SECTION FOUR: APPROACHES TO SOCIAL CARE AND SOCIAL WORK

A range of theories address the way social care work and social work is practiced. This section explores some of these theories and models.

Reading this section, you will learn more about:

- Community work
- Systems theories
- Family group conferencing
- Task centred practice
- Crisis intervention

FURTHER READING

This handbook provides an introduction to the main theories of social care. For further more detailed information on the areas covered in this section, see the following:

- Doel, M. and Marsh, P. (1992) *Task Centred Social Work.* (Aldershot) Ashgate.

- Dominelli, L. (2006) *Women and Community Action.* (London) Policy Press.

- James, R. and Gilliland, B. (2005) *Crisis Intervention Strategies.* Fifth Edition. (Belmont, CA) Brooks/Cole.

- Kanel, K. (2003) *A Guide to Crisis Intervention.* (Pacific Grove, CA) Brooks/Cole.

- Twelvetrees, A. (2001) *Community Work.* Third Edition. Practical Social Work Series. BASW (Basingstoke) Palgrave.

COMMUNITY WORK

Almost 50 years ago the Younghusband Report (1959) identified that there were three main approaches in social work – individual casework, group work and community work. Following this report, community work developed considerably as a model of social work practice. However, in the 1990s community work in the UK became more sidelined as a social work/social care approach and the emphasis moved to individual case work with some group work. Perhaps the exception to this is Scotland, where community work has consistently been a popular approach in social work/social care work.

It could be argued that community work is once again becoming more popular with social inclusion initiatives such as the Surestart programme. The National Occupational Standards for Social Work also make regular reference to work with communities.

It is interesting to note that in many other European countries and in most other continents, community work has remained an influential method of social work. With a number of overseas recruits into the profession, ideas around community work are once again being discussed in the social care/social work arena.

A range of theories are used within community work practice. Community work tends to focus on two main areas – social issues (including social inclusion, social justice etc) and education. The chosen theory base generally depends on the focus of the particular work. There are however, a range of models and approaches which are common to both social and educational community work agendas.

Thomas (1983) identified five main approaches involved in community work:

- Community action
- Community development
- Social planning
- Community organisation
- Service extension

Community Action

This approach is about promoting collective awareness – encouraging action to challenge structures and systems which might oppress or otherwise disadvantage communities. Thomas argues that in working with communities practitioners should strive to help people develop critical perspectives about the "status quo" and to change the balance of power.

Community Development

This is about promoting self help, community integration and mutual support. The idea is that neighbourhood capacities for problem solving will be developed.

Social Planning

This is about assessing community needs and issues and planning strategies to meet the needs identified. Social planning involves developing a true understanding of communities and mobilising appropriate resources.

Community Organisation

This focuses on ensuring the collaboration of different community and statutory agencies to promote and action joint initiatives.

Service Extension

This is a specific strategy which seeks to extend agency operations and services by making them more relevant and accessible. This includes extending services into the local community and giving these services and the staff who are responsible for them, a physical presence in the neighbourhood. (Smith 2006)

Capacity Building

Whilst Thomas's ideas remain influential, other strands to community work have more recently been developed. For example, ideas about capacity building emerged in the 1990s.

Skinner (1997) defines capacity building as development work designed to strengthen the ability of community organisations and

---

groups to develop their own structures, systems and resources so that they can better define and achieve their own objectives. Groups and organisations should be supported (through training and other development activities) to be able to engage in consultation and planning, to manage community projects and to take part in partnerships and community enterprises (Skinner 1997:p2).

Participation and Empowerment

In a Joseph Rowntree Foundation research report, David Wilcox (1994) highlights the importance of community participation and empowerment in community work. He outlines 10 key ideas about community participation, which in many ways mirror the approaches outlined by Thomas (1983):

1. Level of participation – Wilcox identifies a "ladder" of levels of participation (see following).
2. Initiation and process – participation doesn't just happen, it needs to be initiated and should have a clear process.
3. Control – the person/organisation initiating participation is in a strong position to decide how much control to give to others and how much to keep themselves.
4. Power and purpose – Wilcox highlights the importance of community workers understanding empowerment, power and powerlessness.
5. Clarity about the role of the practitioner – practitioners need to continually review their role in community work: could people in the community take on aspects of the role?
6. Stakeholders and community – anyone who has a stake in what happens is a "stakeholder". Some stakeholders will have more influence than others in communities. This should be recognised in any community initiative.
7. Partnership – Wilcox asserts that partnership is a much abused term. Partners must trust each other and share some commitment. Achieving partnership takes time.
8. Commitment – people are committed when they want to achieve something and when clear processes for partnership and empowerment are in place.
9. Ownership of ideas – people are more likely to be committed if they have a sense of ownership.
10. Confidence and capacity – to develop confidence, people may need training.

Ladder of Participation

The most influential aspect of Wilcox's work is the ladder of participation. He suggests a five rung ladder of participation relating to community development and community work more widely.

- Information – which involves merely telling people what is planned (for their community).
- Consultation – this involves offering a few options and listening to feedback, new ideas are not allowed.
- Deciding together – this involves encouraging additional options and ideas and providing opportunities for joint decision making.
- Acting together – this involves various parties working in partnership not only to decide on what action should take place – but also to carry the action out.
- Supporting independent community interests – this involves local groups and organisations being provided with support (which may or may not include the provision of funds) so that they can develop their own agendas.

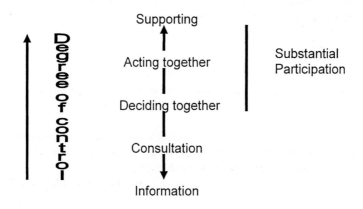

Wilcox points out that information giving and consultation are often presented as being participation. He argues that community participation and effective community work practice involves more than the simple provision of information.

Animation

Literally taken, the word "animation" means bringing something to life. This approach which originates in France, is about bringing life to communities. Animation is predominantly used in community work by those with a focus on education. However, its popularity in community development more generally is growing.

Animation is basically about motivation. Working with an animation approach practitioners try to motivate communities, using a range of methods:

"Animation is that stimulus to the mental, physical and emotional life of people in a given area which moves them to undertake a wider range of experiences through which they find a higher degree of self-realisation, self-expression and awareness of belonging to a community which they can influence."

(Smith 1999)

Practitioners using an animation approach are referred to as animators or animateurs (a French word because animation is a very influential approach in France). They often employ techniques of experiential education and community arts.

Timescales

Developing an understanding about the approaches needed in community work clarifies that it is a long term process:

"Community development takes time. Disadvantaged communities have to be persuaded to participate and their natural suspicion leads them to hang back until there is something to show."

(Glass 2005 in Smith 2006)

Application to Practice

Whilst most social care workers probably won't have the opportunity to engage in community work, there are a range of applications to everyday practice. For example, understanding the ladder of participation can help in recognising methods of engagement and partnership at any level. It can also help to understand how whole communities can experience aspects of exclusion, in any work with individuals. As a practitioner working with individuals, having an understanding of community development methods can also help where you may be able to refer people to particular community projects.

SYSTEMS THEORIES WITHIN SOCIAL CARE PRACTICE

Like many theories, systems theory has at its heart a straightforward claim. For systems theory one of the key starting points is that no person is an island. Everyone has contact with other people. Some of the people are family, some friends and others are people who represent an organisation. The relationships we have with all these people and organisations form a web (or system) around us. The system around us should sustain us and enrich us. There should be a sense of harmony, balance or smooth working in our system.

Systems theory recognises that a person's support network can be placed under strain due to a change in circumstances. This change may be a new event (e.g.: acquired disability of the service user or close family member) or the change could be something progressive. The new or increased strain results in the system not working smoothly; it will loose its sense of balance. By mapping a person's whole system, the professional should be able to work out the source of the system overload. To enable the person's system to operate smoothly, an individual or agency may need to be introduced (either short or long term) to balance the system again. In this way, systems theory is not personal. It does not seek to label the service user or family members.

The Social Care Institute for Excellence considers that systems theory is relevant to social care because:

- It describes and explains the recurring patterns of behaviour found in families, groups and organisations.
- It concentrates on the relationship between the parts rather than parts in isolation.
- Linear thinking, a straightforward cause and effect approach, is a common approach to analysing problems.
- Systemic thinking, however, offers a different perspective: there are multiple causes and effects involved and we, noticing the problem, are actively involved as a part of the problem and its solutions.

(SCIE 2004:p18)

In their work on systems theory Pincus and Minahan (1973) suggested that society and people operate within three systems:

- Informal systems that include family, friends, neighbours and work colleagues; these provide advice and emotional support and also contribute to our sense of worth and personal functioning.
- Formal systems that include clubs and societies, trade unions and other types of groups that can provide support.
- Public systems that include the police, council and local government services, hospitals and schools. These systems tend to have service related functions and duties and powers in their delivery to the community.

It can be suggested that when people are experiencing difficult or traumatic times they will turn to the above systems for support and assistance to help them overcome the problems. Systems theory offers the view that when people are confronted with challenges which they are not able to resolve within their support system they experience conflict and difficulties.

This is the stage at which social care practitioners may intervene and support people to address their presenting needs. Through direct work and applying a problem solving and supporting approach social care workers can develop a work plan and design and implement services through effective partnership working with the service user.

The requirement is for the practitioner to assess the underlying problems and what has led to them being manifested. This will also include the need to consider the personal issues, structural forces and any disadvantage that the service user has experienced.

Pincus and Minahan (1973) also developed a framework for practitioners to use within the helping relationships to resolve the difficulties. The model highlights the need for the social care practitioner to locate the cause of the problem and what impact the problem is having on the system.

The model refers to four aspects of the system and any intervention.

- The "change agent system". This refers to the social care worker and the agency they are representing; it may also include both voluntary and statutory intervention.
- The "client system" focuses on the service user and their system.
- The "target system" makes reference to the desired outcomes.

- The "action system" is the work that is agreed between the service user and the social care practitioner to resolve the identified issues.

Systems theory has been widely used within social work and social care. Family therapy services have placed significant value on seeing the family as a whole and considering how they interact with each other within their family system.

In adult services, systems theory has been extensively used to maximise support for people. Often this focuses on immediate family (carers) and the involvement of health and social care professionals or services to either fill gaps or to sustain relationships (service user/carer relationship) that are under strain.

In learning disability services, systems theory is at the heart of person centred planning. Services should cultivate the opportunity for the service user to establish a range of informal and formal systems.

The analogy of the car breaking down is perhaps a good example of a system and how it interacts. When your car breaks down, often you will check key areas of the engine; this may include the battery, oil and petrol levels. The car is dependant on the battery to start it; it also needs oil to keep the engine working and petrol to make it go. Consequently a system is dependant on key areas for successful maintenance - how a person lives and manages within their system is important for effective functioning.

An alternative way to view systems theory is to focus on the aspect of balance. The worker draws up a list of difficulties the service user is facing as well as positive aspects of their life (e.g.: supportive relationships). If the list of difficulties or problems is longer than the positive aspects, then the worker needs to introduce more positive aspects to try to re-establish a balanced system. A mock example is:

Difficulties	Positive Aspects

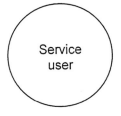

Difficulties

- Poverty

- Vulnerability to abuse or domestic violence

- Limited social network

Positive Aspects

- Minimise benefit claim (contact with advice worker)
- Possibility of entering employment? (Contact with Connexions)
- Develop assertiveness skills
- Inform person of rights (by contact with specialist agency; summons network etc)
- Contact with police
- Support to attend clubs or societies that reflect the person's interests etc (but be specific)

The benefit of this diagrammatic representation is that social environmental aspects can be included (e.g.: poverty, unsuitable housing etc) as well as relationships with people and agencies.

Application to Practice

Systems theory is not without its critics, commentators have suggested that it ignores the diversity of black and minority ethnic communities because it does not address the causes and effects of structural inequality.

However, systems theory is useful since it does express a basic human truth. We all rely on others to one extent or another. By looking at people's systems (support networks) we are able to recognise the strengths that people have.

Often workers support the service user to list or draw their own support systems (this is called an eco-map). There are various benefits to this including:

- Conveys sense of partnership working
- Affirms the service users sense of identity
- Assists the service user recognise the support they have

As well as the individuals who support a service user, as workers, we need to have an awareness of the other factors that have an impact on a person.

FAMILY GROUP CONFERENCES

The last two decades have seen the emergence of Family Group Conferences within children and young peoples social care services in the United Kingdom. The Family Group Conference (herein referred to as FGC) emanated from New Zealand as a practice response to concern that Maori families were experiencing discrimination in the child care system. They can be viewed as a direct application of systems theory.

The UK organisation the Family Rights Group has championed the use of Family Group Conferences within children and young people's social services. This organisation defines the FGC as a:

"A way of giving families the chance to get together to try and make the best plan possible for their children"

In her work on FGC Morris (1995) offers the following commentary:

"A Family Group Conference is a decision making process - it focuses on who plans and how they plan. The model can be used in any circumstances that involve the need to plan for a child."

The definition of a family within the FGC model needs to be considered within a broad context. This needs to recognise the diversity of relationships that occur within families and the tendency amongst many families to have increased contact and support with relatives during difficult times (McGlone et al, 1998).

Within the context of the Children Act 1989 and subsequent legislation there is a clear legal definition of who has parental responsibility for their children. This needs to be considered and assessed when a social care practitioner is planning to use the FGC model as a method of support and intervention.

Central to the practice of FGCs is the notion that families are capable of making decisions about their needs. FGCs are principally aimed at enhancing and encouraging the effective functioning of families. This is uniquely achieved by integrating the families' strengths and utilising them within a problem solving process, which can also be seen as a mechanism for supporting self determination.

Family and kinship members can use the FGC experience as a forum for learning about strengths of their members and mechanisms for supporting each other on a practical and emotional level.

The FGC Model

The FGC process can be broken down into 5 key stages:

- Stage 1 (Referral) - there needs to be an identified need and consequently a plan to address the presenting needs. At this stage a co-ordinator is appointed who is independent of the family and the social care agency. It is also important to consider the cultural needs of the family.

- Stage 2 - The co-ordinator, in consultation with the child and family, issues invitations, agrees venues, dates and timing of the family meeting. The co-ordinator also prepares the participants.

- Stage 3 - At the start of the meeting the co-ordinator chairs the information sharing. Professionals explain their roles, responsibilities, any concerns and available resources

- Stage 4 - Private planning time for the family. The co-ordinator and professionals withdraw whilst the family agree a plan, which should include a contingency plan and review arrangements.

- Stage 5 - The co-ordinator and professionals rejoin the family/kinship and hear the plan. Resources are negotiated and the plan agreed.

It is relevant to note that the plan should not place the child or young person at any risk, the plan should address the concerns and lead to an improved outcome and support plan to ensure the well being and development of the child/young person.

The child or young person who is the subject of the FGC should be encouraged to attend (if they wish to). For children who are not able to attend due to age or development the family should consider that they discuss the needs of the child and that the plan is child centred.

FGCs can be used within adult services, the model lends itself to care planning and community care services for older people. The strengths of the model lie with the concept of partnership working, that families have the fundamental right and responsibility to fully participate in any decisions that may affect them.

FGC can be used in a broad area of practice ranging from children and young people who are defined as in need (s17 of The Children Act 1989), young people leaving care, looked after children, and children and young people and their carers.

It is recognised that Family Group Conferences should not be used during sexual abuse investigations within the family due to the risk of collusion.

Within Youth Offending and Youth Inclusion Support Projects FGCs have developed as an effective tool. The model has been applied within the restorative youth justice process by involving the extended family and kinship. Family group conferences and family decision making meetings have also been successful in victim and offender mediation.

Youth Offending Teams and agencies that have a preventative role seek to address the underlying factors that lead to offending and to developing a plan to address the needs in a holistic manner. Working in this way the aim is to divert children and young people away from the criminal justice and anti social behaviour 'career' pathway.

FGCs are not an alternative to Child Protection Conferences where there are issues of significant harm; it can be an effective supporting mechanism within the child protection plan or core assessment action planning.

There are some clear distinct practice advantages for a social care worker when working with the FGC process:

- The approach promotes partnership and places the child at the centre
- Research indicates that FGC are more successful in getting wider family participation than child protection case conferences
- FGCs are empowering because they actively encourage and enable the family to act as decision makers
- FGC is a universal model which does not have any implicit or structural discrimination base, it can be adapted and modified to meet a varying range of circumstances.

- The approach promotes participation and effective involvement and can challenge the view that society holds about social work intervention.

There has been a substantial amount of work and research which concludes that the FGC meeting promotes effective outcomes for children and young people. The evidence base supports effective anti-discriminatory practice with families from black or minority ethnic communities as it validates the families own social and cultural values, (Tapsfield 2003 and Burford and Hudson 2000).

Family Group Conferences are now used in more than 60 local authorities in England and Wales and in over 20 countries worldwide.

Barnardos 2006 (online) offer the following comments on the outcomes from Family Group Conferences:

- plans are viewed as safe by families and workers in over 90% of conferences
- significantly improved communication and understanding between agencies and families
- a reduction in the number of children who are accommodated and increased contact for children and young people with their family network and friends

TASK CENTRED PRACTICE

Task centred practice was developed by Reid and Shyne in 1969 (Higham 2005) it evolved from a general concern that in depth social care practice was not achieving the same outcomes for service users as short term intervention.

In the early part of the 1960s Perlman recognised that social case work needed to be given some recognition within the context of the emerging social work profession. A cornerstone of Perlman's work was the belief and understanding that within human development there is a need for people to set and accomplish tasks to enable them to develop effective management and coping strategies.

It was largely developed by social work practitioners and educationalists to support the thinking that long term intervention was not as practical both in terms of the worker/service user relationship and the cost effectiveness of social care services. This was because it became clear that the first six to twelve weeks of social work involvement were the most productive in terms of service user responsiveness. After this 'diminishing returns' set in very rapidly, meaning that continuing progress was very gradual and sometimes minimal.

In essence long term case work was questioned and the thinking changed to that of supporting service users in a time limited manner rather than long term intervention that did not appear to promote any change or improved outcomes.

Task centred practice is essentially concerned with assisting people to develop problem solving skills to their presenting difficulties and develop strategies to overcome them and move forward. At the heart of this model is partnership working between the service user and the social care practitioner. The approach assists the worker and service user to consider what the presenting issues are and develop a task setting approach to the helping relationship. Doel and Marsh (1992) offer the following interpretation of task centred practice:

"Task centred practice is a forward thinking, goal orientated approach to social work"

The model is recognised as an appropriate tool for social care workers to use in the following circumstances with service users:

- Personal conflict
- Dissatisfaction in social relationships
- Difficulty in role performance and functioning
- Emotional reactions to a stressful life event
- Limited resources, poverty, poor housing, unemployment
- Behavioral problems that are not assessed as psychological definitions

[Payne (1997), the original list was developed by Reid (1978)]

Whilst this list is not exhaustive care should be taken by practitioners to assess the presenting needs of the service user and discuss the plan to work with the service user using this method.

Time should be taken to explore with the service user what the method promotes and how it can support the service user to develop solutions to their problems. You should also ensure that there is a clear understanding between the worker and the service user on what the problem is, this promotes greater clarity and will focus the work.

What is distinctive within task centred practice is that the worker and the service user agree the problem and then consider specific tasks to deal with the issues. To maximise the likelihood that this approach will work, the service users own priorities must be worked on (that's what makes it a person centred approach). If the service user lacks insight and suggests trivial problems to work on, then this approach may not be any good. One of the perceived benefits of task centred work is that the social care staff may not need to 'pry' into a person's life. It is the present situation and what to do about it that counts.

A key aspect of task centred work is that it is the service user who addresses the problem, who carries out the work (not the worker). This is because the approach is seeking to support the service user develop skills to address difficulties. If the same or similar difficulties arise in the future, the service user should be able to address them by themselves without needing to fall on social care staff. Built into the worker and service user relationship is the tenet of review and evaluation. For example, if limited progress is being made then this should be discussed and reflected on within the sessions.

Task centred practice has five key stages that are often referred to as phases (Ford and Postle 2000). These phases should be followed within a structured approach to appointments or sessions with service users and you should plan for no more than 12 meetings. However this will depend on the progress and the presenting problems that the service user is looking to overcome.

The stages can be broken down into the following key sections in direct work to support service users to achieve their goals:

1. Problem Exploration. The social care worker and the service user use this time to discuss the problems and consider which issues they want to deal with first.

2. Agreement. There should be a shared understanding between the service user and practitioner about what the problem is and how they are going to target and action plan. This phase is also referred to as the selecting and prioritising of problems.

3. Formulating an objective. This phase involves setting goals and making a contract between the worker and service user. The contract should also reflect the arrangements for the worker and service user to meet with deadlines.

   Care should be taken by the worker to ensure that the problems that have been identified to work on do not overwhelm the service user. They should be achievable and realistic.

4. Achieving the tasks or working to implement the tasks. This can be done jointly with the service user in a session or separately. There is also the potential for the worker to undertake any identified advocacy work here.

5. Bringing the work to a conclusion. This is an opportunity to consider what progress has been made and discussion should focus on the outcomes and developments that the service user has made towards their identified goals. This session should aim to be as in depth as possible and should have a reflective focus. You may also want to ask the service user how they feel about the problems now, and what changes have been made.

It is important to remember that if the presenting issues have been resolved the sessions can be finished earlier. However in the event of the issues not being resolved or in the event of emerging problems the worker and the service user can agree to meet for some more sessions. Again these should be time limited.

The Limitations of Task Centred Practice

There is a wealth of evidence that suggests that the task centred approach as a social care method of intervention, is effective and is a tool that is understood by service users (Reid and Epstein 1972).

However, as with any theoretical approach, there are limitations.

Commentators suggest that one of the weaknesses of task centred practice is that it a relatively simple model and should not be seen as the universal underpinning theoretical tool to inform direct work with service users.

Some peoples emotional and life situation is complex and the task centred approach does not easily address complex emotional issues.

A psychodynamic approach would go as far as saying that if deep seated unconscious behaviours (that are limiting a person's social functioning) are not addressed through counselling or therapy, then lists of tasks are in danger of being irrelevant. The person won't do them, they will act in ways consistent with their unconscious directions.

Some practitioners have found the drawing up of an agreement or contract problematic [stage or phase 3 in Ford and Postle's (2000) list]. It has been claimed that drawing up a contract can come across as disempowering. Since the tasks should be for the service user to do, it can come across as setting homework for the service user which will be 'marked' by the social care worker (teacher) the next time they meet. There are counter arguments to this, such as the agreement or contract ensures there is clarity and entering into agreements (of some form) is commonly done by adults (e.g.: job contract). However, the criticism does have some merit.

Task centred practice is often misunderstood by social care staff. It is commonly assumed it is the worker who does all the tasks (e.g.: contact the local housing agency). No. That's cheating! The work for the social care staff consists of supporting the service user to recognise they have the skills, or support them to develop the skills and confidence to do the task for themselves. When the service user does this, it is self reinforcing (both in terms of an issue or problem is resolved and they did it themselves).

In spite of its limitations, task centred practice is likely to be a staple theory in the practice of many social care and social work staff.

Application to Practice

In summary the use of task centred practice is an effective method to use with service users who are willing and keen to promote change. It has a strong ethos of partnership working with service users giving them the opportunity to seek resolution to their problems. Task centred work has contributed to practice in several service areas that include front line social care teams and project based services. The method also reinforces people's strengths and the underlying ability of people to recover and make changes that are core values of social care.

CRISIS INTERVENTION

Within day to day practice with service users, workers will encounter situations where individuals or families are experiencing traumatic times or crisis points within their lives.

There is a need for social care practitioners to understand this within the context of the helping relationship.

Some people cope well with crises on their own and do not require any intervention or services, some people will seek support from their families or network of friends within their communities. Whereas other people may turn to the supporting agencies for emotional and practical support at the point of their crisis.

It is relevant to consider that there is a difference between stress and crisis, each individual person will respond differently to presenting difficulties.

During a person's life they will experience a range of issues that can have an impact on them at both an emotional and psychological level that leaves them feeling overwhelmed and not able to manage.

These life stage events can be varied and may include bereavement, a break up of a relationship, abuse, violence both within the family and within the community, unemployment and child birth.

It is important to consider the definition of the term crisis, it has been difficult to locate a universal definition however Bard and Ellison, 1974 (cited in Stepney and Ford 2000) offer the following commentary:

"Crisis is a subjective reaction to a stressful life experience, one so affecting the stability of the individual that the ability to cope or function may be seriously compromised"

At the heart of this model is that it is an approach that aims to support service users to regain control of their lives by learning or re-establishing coping skills so that they can move forward after the presenting issues have been dealt with and the crisis has been resolved. There is a clear expectation of time limited involvement.

Stages of the Crisis

Caplan (1965), one of the first writers to discuss crisis intervention, considered that crisis have three phases:

- impact stage
- recoil stage
- adjustment and adaptation stage

Golan (1974) (cited in Coulshed and Orme 1998) also followed the three stage approach but called them (somewhat unimaginatively):

- beginning
- middle
- end

The time frame from beginning to end is about 6 to 8 weeks. To follow the stages could be something like this:

1. A crisis arises and has some impact on a person. It could be bereavement, major loss, active threat of homelessness etc.

   The person's own coping skills are overwhelmed by the current crisis. Hence social work services may become involved.

   The individual may experience a series of feelings and emotional responses that leads them to feel low and vulnerable. Golan, in her work identifies this as the "active crisis ".

   At this stage it is important for the social care worker to have an understanding of the emotional responses that are being displayed by the service user; these could include anger, hostility, confrontation and sadness. The range of emotional responses will vary and depend on the presenting issues that have precipitated the crisis.

   The values the social worker or social care worker brings into the relationship are crucial, given how vulnerable the service user could be. Aspects of professional values include:

   - Most (all?) people experience difficult and dangerous episodes that will lead to a sense of vulnerability. At such time, requiring more support is common (and in many ways the rational thing to do.)

- Even though the crisis may have been unwanted and unexpected, basic values include a recognition that people have:

    - the ability for growth and development
    - a level of understanding into their own needs
    - the ability to solve their presenting difficulties and problems

2. The recoil stage. This refers to the conscious, planned responses the service user can make. Even though the service user is in a crisis, it is important the social worker or social care worker uses a structured approach. For a social worker, this includes all the established care management and assessment skills. This planning stage should acknowledge that the workers involvement is time limited.

3. Adjustment and adaptation/End Stage. For the service user, their emotional responses may still be strongly felt. However, they should be able to function. The need for service intervention should have receded, therefore the worker can withdraw.

Roberts (2005) in his work on crisis management and intervention highlighted a framework that identified seven key areas for workers to work within:

- Assessing lethality and safety needs
- Establishing rapport with the service user by using key counselling skills of clear communication and non-judgmental approach and respect.
- Highlighting the presenting problems and any previous coping mechanisms utilised by the service user. Evaluate the effectiveness of these mechanisms.
- Supporting the service user to deal with the anxiety and stress by engaging them in active dialogue in a safe environment that promotes confidentiality.
- Supporting the service user to explore the situation and consider what changes need to be made to enable them to deal with the problem more effectively.

- Developing an action plan. Provide constructive and positive feedback to the service user on their motivation to face up to the problems and deal with them.
- Follow up support or advice on services that could be available in the future.

(Roberts 2005)

Application to Practice

Crisis intervention as a method of social care intervention for workers has distinct links to task centred work. Crisis intervention is a tool that can be utilised by workers in a broad range of case situations ranging from working with older people with mental health needs, to children and young people who are looked after. It can also be a relevant method to employ with people who have experienced trauma.

A strong understanding and commitment to anti-oppressive practice is required by workers when engaging with service users. Crisis intervention approaches need to be delivered within the context of person centred care and have a clear commitment by the worker to promote and enable the service user as an autonomous and independent person.

There will of course be occasions where service users will present a risk to themselves and others, at this stage there will need to be a continuous assessment of the risk and where appropriate statutory intervention may be required to secure the safety and wellbeing of the service user.

SECTION FIVE: WORKING IN ORGANISATIONS

All social care workers work in an organisation. They also work with a range of other organisations. Understanding organisations is therefore an important aspect of a social care workers knowledge.

Reading this section, you will learn more about:

- Management Theory
- Organisational Theory
- Multi agency and Multi Disciplinary working
- Team working

FURTHER READING

This handbook provides an introduction to the main theories of social care. For further more detailed information on the areas covered in this section, see the following:

- Barrett, G., Sellman, D. and Thomas, J. (eds). (2005) *Interprofessional Working in Health and Social Care* (Basingstoke) Palgrave.

- Hornby, S. and Atkins, J. (2000) *Collaborative Care: Interprofessional, interagency and interpersonal.* Second edition. (Oxford) Blackwell Science.

- Huxham, C. and Vangen, D. (2005) *Managing to Collaborate: The theory and practice of collaborative advantage.* (London) Routledge.

- Payne, M. (2004) *Teamwork in Multiprofessional Care.* (Basingstoke) Palgrave Macmillan.

- Weinstein, J., Whittington, C. and Leiba, T. (eds) (2003) *Collaboration in Social Work Practice.* (London) Jessica Kingsley.

- Wilson, F. (2004) *Organisational Behaviour and Work: A Critical Introduction.* (Oxford) Oxford University Press.

MANAGEMENT THEORY

There are as many theories of management as there are management consultants. Each management consultant has her or his own approach which they claim 'works'.

Given the quantity of management theories this section will therefore be selective. Some of the traditional management theories will be discussed as well as some of the more recent approaches that focus on change and leadership.

Managing a Service or Team

One of the classic management theories is McGregor's X and Y Theory (McGregor, 1960). In this McGregor argued that managers approach their staff with a set of basic assumptions.

Theory X assumptions include:-

- Staff do not actually like to work. They only turn up for work because they need the money.
- Staff will not work hard and will seek to avoid responsibility and personal initiative.
- Staff will only work hard when they are clearly directed as to what to do and are continually monitored.

Theory Y assumptions include:-

- People actually sense that work is as much a part of life as rest and recreation.
- Staff who enjoy their work will develop a loyalty to the organisation.
- Staff are not only able to accept responsibility but some staff actually want responsibility.
- Drawing on staff members own ideas and creativity can benefit the organisation.

Whilst these assumptions about staff have aspects that are caricatured or stereotyped there has been a degree of acceptance that in large, mass production organisations theory X is more relevant, partly because theory Y is difficult to apply.

However theory Y is considered to be relevant to organisations where there is a commitment from staff to the organisation's objectives. Where staff are able to apply self direction and autonomy then they can work better than if they had been carrying out specific directed instructions.

In this sense theory Y calls on managers to consult with staff, maximise staff participation and support staff responsibility. Within social care this should smoothly feed into support staff and senior support staff involving service users in planning the care they receive.

There is further indirect support for the theory Y approach in findings by White et al (2003). In care services in which abuse had occurred there appeared to be a management style that was autocratic and controlling. This management approach generated a service ethos or culture that influenced how care staff acted towards service users and how more independent service users acted towards vulnerable service users (by being controlling and abusive).

Given how old McGregor's theory is why mention it? Because so many social care services are still managed in a directive style where consultation and participation are non existent or tokenistic! Directive management styles are arguably able to still exist in social care because so many staff quickly build up a commitment to service users and immediate colleagues and therefore endure autocratic and directive managers. Also some managers can find that consultation and participation take more time and slow down decision making.

Within social care the need to develop person centred care will mean that immediate support workers and senior support workers should have greater autonomy, so that in consultation with other relevant people, they can seek to ensure that service users have the support that they need. This will mean that management styles that cultivate staff responsibility are more likely to deliver good, flexible care.

Argyris (1964) has gone on to describe organisations in terms of theory X and theory Y. Theory X organisations are pyramid structures that have high levels of bureaucracy. Working relationships are characterised by:-

- Low levels of trust
- Human relationships which focus on getting the job done
- A strong culture of direction, authority and control

- Rewards and penalties closely relate to achieving the organisations goal
- There is no 'safe' environment that allows initial evaluation
- The organisation has within itself intergroup conflict, rigidity and mistrust. When something goes wrong the organisation's ability to solve the problem is impaired.

By contrast Argyris characterises humanistic and democratic organisations (Theory Y) as:-

- Able to treat people as human beings
- Recognise the individuals need to influence their own work and the organisations
- Expecting that people can develop further - which is encouraged
- Encouraging human relationships to be honest. This includes addressing unconscious attitudes so they can be discussed and controlled
- Valuing intergroup co-operation and flexibility – this is viewed as enhancing the organisations effectiveness

The implications of Argyris' model for social care organisations are clear. There should be a culture within the organisation that welcomes the creative contribution of staff at all levels. Again one of the aspirations in social care is that this ethos will filter down so that care staff seek to maximise the contribution of service users in their own care (and in the general development of the service).

The benefit of honesty within organisations is also one of Argyris' points. Within social care organisations, it is not clear that they are as honest as they can and should be. There is anecdotal evidence that by trying to meet targets and satisfy inspection requirements, honesty has been stretched.

Motivation

In the last half of the 20th Century management theory spent time addressing the issue of motivation.

Maslow's hierarchy of needs (which is addressed in Volume One of this two volume series) has often been referred to, especially the higher stages relating to self-actualisation. Self-actualisation can just refer to a person's aspirations to be as good a worker as possible. Other management writers have also developed their own viewpoints. McClelland (e.g.: 1961) has argued that there are some people who have a need for achievement and this need can be identified and drawn upon in organisations.

McClelland has claimed that people with the need to achieve choose targets for themselves that are neither too easy nor too difficult and unobtainable. Achievers select a target that will stretch them and in its own way is personally demanding, but which can be attained.

Achievement motivated people are primarily motivated by the desire to succeed at their task. Whilst they will not turn down financial rewards they are not solely motivated by money.

Achievement motivated people like pragmatic feedback, that is to know how well they are doing at their job. They are not so concerned about how much their colleagues like them.

Achievement motivated people have a good chance of becoming managers. However it is not clear that they will automatically make good managers. Since they are so committed to achievement and expect to set demanding (but attainable) personal targets they can often expect the same of others, but not everyone in a team wants to be personally stretched. Therefore managers who are achievement motivated need to ensure they can use people skills to get the most out of their team. Some staff prefer a sense of being liked to enable them to perform to an acceptable level rather than receiving feedback that they have solved a problem.

Service Performance or Staff Care?

One of the balancing acts of management is to ensure that the staff team or service actually performs as it should do whilst also giving the individual team members a sense that managers want what is best for them, in terms of professional and personal development.

In care services the need to manage these two aspects is particularly striking. As a care service we often work with vulnerable people. Service users have often been excluded and so it is very important that the service they receive is sensitive to the service users needs and gives them a sense of being wanted and valued. Staff do have to perform the whole range of care tasks well.

Since we work in social care (or health care) then there is an expectation that staff will be supported by the organisation when needed. This has resulted in local authorities providing staff with various benefits.

In one social care service a manager became concerned that it had turned on its head. It appeared to become a service that benefited staff (first) and service users a poor second. Staff sickness rates were high. Some staff appeared to make the most of local authority sickness benefits. Using relief staff (or just running the service each day with minimum staffing) meant that service users had basic care and poor continuity.

This dilemma, of having a concern for service performance and a concern for team members was recognised by Blake and Mouton (1968) who developed a managerial grid. This grid is made up of four quarters.

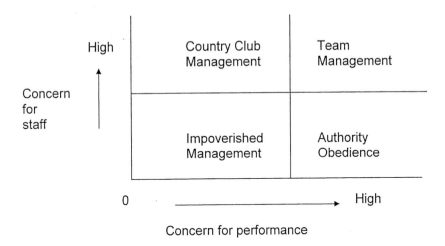

The four boxes relate to:

1) Impoverished Management. Here, managers exert the minimum effort, both in terms of concern for people and having a poor focus on performance.

2) Authority – Obedience. The focus on performance is very strong. There is little time given to concern for staff. The organisation

may arrange conditions of work so that human elements interfere to a minimal extent.

3) Country Club Management. Attention to the needs of colleagues and staff is high, organisations may have a friendly reputation. However, there is a danger that staff comfort may be a higher priority than organisational performance.

4) Team Management. The staff are committed to the aims of the organisation. Mutual support and co-operation are seen as desirable for their own benefit and it results in a more effective organisation.

This model has been so popular that questionnaires have been developed so that individuals can identify which type of management style they have. The intention is to encourage managers to work towards having the skills of a team manager.

The implications for managing social care (or health) services are immediate. Managers will need to be explicit about their intention, that they want a positive supportive environment for staff and a service that performs.

Managers may find it helpful to adopt a dual track approach.

- Identify and list management and organisational expectations and actions that support staff
- Identify and list expectations and actions around service performance
- Be open and honest with your staff team

Leadership and Managing Change

For a number of reasons, classic models of management were presented as being fairly objective. Management was about establishing a system and then just maximising its efficiency. From the 1920s onwards, alternative views were expressed (e.g.: Elton Mayo, 1933). Since then there have been an increasing number of writers such that the dominant theme in modern management theory is how to respond to change and enable the organisation to adapt. One of the key management skills, in harnessing the skills in the organisation and changing to meet societal needs, is leadership. The change in language is quite intentional, the different words generate completely different images of how the manager should make their presence felt. Rather than listing all the different leadership and management writers (since there are many), some of the common themes include:

- Developing a clear vision for the future direction of the organisation. Leadership shows <u>how</u> the vision is generated. A key quality of leadership is that it articulates the goals and hopes of the people who will be expected to apply it. Therefore, the leader must consult. Listen before declaring the direction. The more people feel involved in a major decision, the more likely they are to apply it.

  Then the vision needs to be conveyed. Memos don't work! The leader must be seen, they must talk about it with enthusiasm. They need to be able to convey to colleagues how changes will affect them and how they will be supported through the changes. The leader will need to have a team or alliance which has a key role in promoting the vision.

- The vision needs to have an ethical aspect or convey values. It is one of the means by which people will be motivated.
- Leadership involves leading by example [if the focus is on management, this concept (of leading by example) is too often lost]. Leading by example includes aspects of personal remuneration, as well as the quality of relationships the leader has with colleagues and the people who have contact with the organisation.
- The leader needs to show that they accept responsibility. When it comes to making decisions, they will make them and will not avoid the consequences.
- Risk taking is part of leadership.
- Due to complexity of work situations, a senior manager cannot know everything. Therefore the manager shows leadership by drawing on the talents of others. Leadership is about cultivating and welcoming the strengths that others bring – and attributing credit where it is due.
- Leadership includes having standards, what is acceptable and not acceptable. Targets should be set for an ethical or value reason and so should be achieved for that reason as well.

Implications for Practice

The rise of the importance of leadership skills in management should be welcomed in social care (and health) organisations. Social care services are going through an extended period of change; therefore the leadership qualities a manager brings can help ensure the changes are positively applied. Where changes are required, it's clear that one person cannot force them through. There needs to be a core team of people who are enthusiastic about the changes. The changes should have a clear sense of being located within social care values.

The leadership skills include being seen and leading by example. Frontline managers should never lose their ability to engage positively with service users.

ORGANISATIONAL THEORY

In origin, the organisation was created since it was realised that 100 people given specific roles with the shared goal of performing a task would achieve that goal more successfully than if the 100 people were working independently (but still aiming for the same goal).

One of the basic features of an organisation is that specialisation of roles is required. This immediately resulted in a fragmentation of the work tasks. Most individuals will only learn their own particular job role. The power of the individuals who arrange the organisation is enhanced, both because they allocate tasks in the first place and because they are possibly the only people who have knowledge of the whole process.

Classical Organisational Theory

Two of the key writers about organisational theory were Henri Fayol (1949) and Max Weber (1947). Fayol's (1949) principles of management or organisation included:

- Specialisation of labour
- Focus on work when at work, personal interests to be 'left at the factory gate'
- Remuneration, fair pay for working, job for life for good workers
- A whole range of principles relating to centralised authority, chain of command, discipline etc.

The whole focus of Fayol's approach was very task oriented. The only acknowledgements to a people orientated approach was fair pay and job security.

Max Weber based his organisational principles on his study of bureaucracies. Some of the key characteristics that Weber wrote about include:

- Functional specialisation. Each worker had a specific work role and a clear sense of their responsibilities.
- Clear lines of hierarchial authority. Workers need to know who their boss is and the chain of command must be respected.

- Expert training of managers. This may require trainee managers to spend time in various branches of the organisation so that when they come to manage that branch, they know what is involved.
- Decision making based on rules to ensure consistency. This is supported by extensive use of written documents. All decisions are rational and consistent with the rules.

For many years managers were expected to arrange their organisation in a manner consistent with Weber's prescription.

In contrast to Weber's belief in organisational efficiency and order Selznick (1949) argued that it was futile and idealist to expect organisations to attain Weber's characteristics. Selznick argued that human behaviour in organisations always resulted in a range of effects. There were conflicts and individual interpretation of rules that resulted in inconsistencies.

Selznick's critique of organisations continues to be valuable. When services are working with difficult to engage individuals there can often be an organisational or professional approach that is different from the publicly expressed aim of the main decision makers.

One example of this is in relation to illegal drug use, the Government policy is clearly focused on reducing drug use and assisting people into rehabilitation programmes. However, this clear focus is blunted since direct support drug workers interpret how this should be applied in a variety of ways. Many workers are concerned that if they try to promote rehabilitation they could alienate the drug user such that the service user does not visit the service again. The worker often waits until the service user shows an interest in rehabilitation themselves.

In probation and youth offending, there is anecdotal evidence that supervision is of variable quality blunting official claims that offenders are assertively challenged to face up to their offending behaviour.

Modern Organisational Theory

This has been referred to as contingency theory. The use of the term contingency means the way an organisation is structured will depend on what its task is, its ability to use technology and environmental factors. These three aspects, tasks, technology and environment will each be looked at in turn.

Task

This has been structured into a matrix by Perrow (1967)

	Few expectations (same product at end)	Many expectations (each end product is different, unique)
Unformed (high level of skill, intuition)	Craft work, pottery, artwork, plumbing, technical support.	Specialist research, film making; aerospace; large, unique tasks e.g. large ships
Formed (open to structured analysis)	Routine manufacturing. The few problems that occur are usually easy to understand.	Custom machinery, engineering production. The application of well known principles and technology to new and different situations.

What the matrix means:

- Bottom left, where tasks have few exceptions and are well understood. This can allow organisations to be centralised and focus on mass production. Little autonomy is necessary. They are bureaucracies.
- Top right. This is the other extreme to the bureaucracies. Each task is new and unique. There needs to be flexibility and a high level of autonomy for staff. Staff are very skilled.

What does this mean to social care? The implications are quite direct. When community care was first introduced into adult services, there was a sense that social workers should recognise the uniqueness of the individual service user, that care plans would express this and the skills of the social worker would be called upon to generate a 'seamless service' around the service user. There was, initially, a belief that there was adequate funding (this is an environmental factor).

If this had carried on, then there would have been pressures to decentralise decision making and services would have formed that were relatively small and provided tailored services.

It quickly became clear that environmental factors (demand for support and funding that is nowhere near adequate to meet the demands) have resulted in adult social services providing a set range of service options. In domiciliary care, the choice is usually between a 15 minute personal care call or a 30 minute personal care call. Due to the need to control budgets, decision making is increasingly centralised, either directly through a senior manager making a decision on an individual case or indirectly by the managers stating where the eligibility threshold is set and then all workers have to apply that in their decision making. Put crudely, social care and social work has been reduced to a mass production process. The mechanistic bureaucracy of social services has resulted in the production of policies and procedures that allow for little variation [e.g.: no lifting of people during personal care, make use of technology (hoists)].

Technology and Task

The implications of technology and the task within organisational theory are also relevant to social care and mirror the process referred to above. Woodward (1965) argued that certain activities will naturally go with certain structures.

a)   Where the product is unique or small in number, the skills and knowledge of the workers are at least as important as the technology. However, the work units are relatively expensive but they can have relatively flat structures (a low percentage of managers).

b)   Where the task is one of mass production, technology can be heavily used which results in a structure that has a huge bottom level, tall hierarchy with a relatively large number of managers; a mechanistic, bureaucratic structure; relatively cheap to operate per worker.

In social care there have often been pilot services started that aim to provide a specialist high quality service. Since it is a pilot service, there are usually only a small number of service users. Such a pilot service corresponds to (a) (above). Examples of the pilot services can be found in children's services, mental health services and learning disability services. In learning disability services in the late 1980s small numbers of service users were moved from long stay hospitals into small community care homes. Often there were significant levels of support from psychology, physiotherapy and other professionals.

Many pilot projects were written up in journals which related the many benefits of the move to small community homes.

When the old long stay hospitals had to speed up the process, it involved far more service users moving to new homes. The quality of the provision noticeably declined since there was far more of a mass production aspect.

In older people's services the pressure of type (b) are strikingly clear. Both now and in the future far more use of technology is being made. At present personal call alarm pendants and telephone ordering of frozen meals are some examples. In the future, remote health and welfare checks will be sent by telephone to staffed offices, while online self assessments for equipment could become common place.

Despite the almost universal rejection of the model of large older people's care homes, there is no sign that such provision will come to an end. Large older peoples care homes are one of the cheapest ways to provide (just) adequate care.

Environment

Organisational theory claims that an organisation that faces complex, uncertain, environments establishes relatively autonomous branches so that each branch of the organisation can address a specific set of challenges. This is termed adaptation.

The process of adaptation can clearly be seen within social work services and social care. Social work services have become increasingly specialised with teams for older people, older people with mental health problems, learning disability teams etc. The same specialisation process has occurred in children's services.

Social care (provider) services have shown similar adaptation. There are care services just for, say, older people with dementia, or adults with mental health problems and alcohol dependency, or adults with autism etc.

Management theory has highlighted that when adaptation occurs (an organisation has several specialist branches) there are difficulties in managing the branches as one organisation. A senior manager may not have had experience of one or more of the specialisms and may not understand the effect planned organisational changes will have on those specialisms. Hence organisations are vulnerable to splitting. One of the branches moves to another organisation.

There is also a process of natural selection. Organisations whose structures do not fit the environment fail. Many new organisations fail in the first few years. This could be for internal or environmental reasons.

Within social care and social work the environment has been going through a process of significant change.

One key environmental factor is Government policy and expectation around care. In many ways the Government has many independent service providers between a hammer and an anvil. The Government has sought to improve standards in the quality of care but, arguably, the fees they are willing to pay have not reflected the increased costs that agencies have to pay to improve quality.

It is not only independent social care agencies that have been affected by the changing environment. Local authorities in England have had to remodel social services by moving children's social work services into a new structure with education. In England, registration and inspection services have been disbanded and reformed every two years since 2002.

Power and Dependency Between Organisations

The nature of dependency and power is also addressed in organisational theory. Every organisation is dependent on suppliers and customers for resources and money. The extent that one organisation is dependent on another will determine its level of power or powerlessness. Hence, if a provider of care services receives most of its work from one local authority contract but that local authority uses five different care providers, then the local authority is the more powerful organisation.

Organisation theory also conveys that dependency is a function of the availability of alternative supply. Hence, a local authority may not be able to exercise much significant power if there are only two or three organisations that can provide home care. However, most local authorities seek to address this by inviting organisations to tender for contracts.

Dependency and power is also a function of how much 'A' needs what 'B' has got. This is most relevant to the service user - organisation relationship. The service user (A) needs personal care. The organisation (B) has the trained staff to provide that care. This will result in A (service user) having a sense of dependency and powerlessness in relation to the organisation (B).

Individuals, groups or other organisations that are in the environment and effect, or are effected by an organisation, are called stakeholders. The stakeholders may, or may not, have the power to influence or protect their interests. Stakeholders may co-operate with each other and so bring increased pressure to bear on the organisation or may even compete against each other.

In social work and social care one of the key stakeholders is the service user. Arguably, the service user is not a powerful stakeholder. Efforts to address this have been made, especially in children's services, by establishing advocacy projects and expectations around involving children and young people in developing care services.

Other stakeholders are often the other statutory organisations e.g.: health, education, housing, police etc. The relative levels of power and influence will vary depending on the specific task being focused on. Hence, if a number of care homes are due to be shut, the influence of the housing department could be significant. If a protection from abuse procedure is being developed, police involvement will be crucial.

MULTI AGENCY AND MULTI DISCIPLINARY WORKING

Surprisingly, very little theory has been generated around multi agency or multi disciplinary working. A great deal has been written around the practical and applied aspects of multi agency or multi disciplinary working.

In this section, we will:

- Clarify various concepts
- Outline some of the practical and applied points
- Discuss the extent of theory relevant to this area

"Multi Agency" and "Multi Disciplinary". What's the Difference?

Multi agency refers to a situation where staff from different organisations seek to work together. The staff could have similar professional backgrounds or could have different professional backgrounds but it is the fact that they are employed by different organisations. One example could be a social worker on a children's team has contact with a worker on the Youth Offending Team. The Youth Offending Team worker could be social work qualified, but their role is different to that of the social worker from the children's team.

Often multi agency working involves staff working together who have different professional backgrounds. To work effectively, there would need to be some understanding of the different perspectives of:

- each agency (or organisation)
- each other's professional viewpoint or specialism

Multi disciplinary working relates to staff working with colleagues who have different professional training and roles. It is common for multi disciplinary teams to be employed by the same organisation and to be based together. In practical terms, this is seen as maximising the benefits of multi disciplinary working.

However, there are other models of multi disciplinary working. Some multi disciplinary teams are all based together but some staff are employed by, say, the local NHS trust and other staff are employed by the local social services department. The main practical issues relate to supervision. The health professionals are supervised by a health manager, the social services professionals are supervised by a social services manager.

Additionally, other models of multi disciplinary working relate to a team of professionals who are from different agencies but are brought together to support a service user. In this sense, the term multi disciplinary working becomes interchangeable with the team multi agency working.

Multi Disciplinary Working: Practical Points

The factors that aid and hinder multi disciplinary working have been well expressed.

Factors that encourage multi disciplinary working include:

- Personal commitment, especially enthusiasm from key managers and senior staff within the multi disciplinary team
- Having a common goal and shared vision
- Clarity of roles and communication. Where possible some projects should be rotated e.g.: facilitating service user group working
- Explicit support from the host organisation

Factors that can hinder multi disciplinary working include:

- Not having a shared base but being dispersed
- Attitudes of team members. Professional hierarchies and feelings of domination may provoke reactions
- Role of professional bodies which seek to safeguard professional standards. It's not clear if some team members would use these claims as a reason or excuse or if there are actual barriers created by professional bodies.

[From Wilson and Pirrie, 2000]

Multi Disciplinary Working and Theory

Warrington et al (2004) argued that much has been written about the promotion of multi agency working and the practical aspects but little theory has been developed. Theory is the attempt to take one step back and to look at broader processes that can be repeated and so lend themselves to potential predictability.

Warrington et al (2004) draws on Engestrom's (1999) use of activity theory. Activity theory relates to two or more organisations, each of which has its own rules, identity and specialisations of labour having contact with each other. Each organisation is trying to achieve their own goals (which may or may not be shared goals). When two or more organisations have contact, this creates an activity system. There are certain principles of the activity system which include:

- The activity system is composed of multiple points of view, some within each respective organisation, some from the staff who have contact with staff from other organisations (the interface). Different professionals also have varied views. The larger the organisation or the more organisations there are, results in more points of view. This potential cacophony (many voices, noises) is both a source of tension and innovation calling for translation and negotiation.
- Organisation's own history. Organisations are the way they are, partly due to their history. There is an accumulated knowledge within an organisation that is often expressed through policies and procedures, authorisation processes etc.
- There are structural tensions and contradictions within an organisation and between organisations when they come into contact with each other. These contradictions are not the same as problems or conflicts. The adoption of new practices, technology or goals often results in a new contradiction. These contradictions generate tensions and disturbances. These can generate conflicts but can also be the spur to introduce additional changes.
- Activity systems go through long cycles of transformation. The transformations are partly driven by the contradictions within the existing activity system. When the number or significance of the contradictions become too great, there is a deliberate collective change effort to establish a new organisation or organisations.

The relevance of this to social work and social care is quite clear. The tensions and contradictions within social care, social work and other agencies are well known. Often service users who have more than one significant need highlight the tensions. Individuals with 'dual diagnosis' which can mean a person with mental health problems and alcohol or drug dependency, have always had difficulty accessing appropriate services. In recent years, specialist workers or specialist teams have been established. However, the move to specialisation has resulted in some service users who 'don't fit neatly into a specialism' being batted from one team to another.

One of the obvious tensions and contradictions is between providing individual person centred care for lots of people (which is expensive) and staying within budgets (which are limited and inadequate). Often re-organisations are planned to improve efficiency and so free money to address the contradictions around person centred care and budgets. However, the re-organisation just introduces other contradictions without solving the key budgetary one.

The whole process of transformation is also very clear and current, as children's services re-orientate themselves so that they are aligned with education services. Even this transformation will not remove contradictions. New ones will emerge and the whole process will start again.

Professional Boundaries: Assets or Dated Barrier?

Much of the literature relating to multi disciplinary working has claimed that effectiveness is maximised by confirming specific areas of professional expertise partly because this minimises conflict. Hence a social worker only needs to know that the service user they are with may benefit from an occupational therapy assessment and leave the rest to the occupational therapist when they visit.

However activity theory would argue that the perspectives and voices being raised within health, social care/social work, education, housing etc, are calling for an end to the procession of professionals who each assess the service user, give additional (and sometimes contradictory) information and leave the service user confused. There needs to be qualitively different forms of professional practice. Workers should take the initiative in re-orientating themselves to work settings characterised by change, distributed expertise (meaning the knowledge is not held just be one professional but by several) and boundary crossing.

Boundary crossing is characterised by the professionals own learning being related to horizontal knowledge (knowledge relevant to the needs of the service users the team has contact with). This is in contrast to vertical knowledge where, say, the social worker learns about aspects of social work practice that may, or may not, have relevance to the service users they have contact with.

Alongside the language of boundary crossing is the term knotworking. This refers to the need for professionals to establish new diagonal ties and connections that aid and enhance the performance of the activity system (but knotworking could also create further contradictions as mentioned earlier).

In many ways, the establishment of multi disciplinary teams in the same office base brings to a head the contradictions and tensions that exist when professionals from different backgrounds work together. Much of the existing writing on multi disciplinary working views boundary crossing and role blurring as a threat and will contribute to professional tensions and anxieties. However, other writers argue that multi disciplinary teams create an opportunity for expansive learning. Some writers (e.g: Atkinson et al 2002) have argued that multi disciplinary working will lead to hybrid professionals who have knowledge of other agencies and professional disciplines.

There are other processes that are heightening the contradiction of maintaining professional boundaries. In multi disciplinary teams, a service user is allocated to a named staff member. However, in some teams if the named staff member is not available (e.g.: annual leave, or off sick) and an issue arises for the service user, then another team member carries out the work that is required. This highlights how the worker needs skills and knowledge relevant to the service user's needs rather than skills and knowledge that are part of a list from a professional qualification.

The need for professionals to be able to question each other has been highlighted by the Victoria Climbié inquiry. We are not expecting social workers to go through doctors training. However, if a professional is to question a colleague from a different professional discipline, then the more background knowledge a worker has the more pertinent their questioning is likely to be.

The early experiments with on line self assessments that have been carried out in respect of older people's services relating to the need for minor adaptations, also illustrates how contradictions arise. Put simply, if a person without any professional background in health and social care can assess some of their own needs, then can't most workers from one of the health and social care professions also assess the person's needs?

Activity theory provides us with a broad theoretical framework that helps us recognise that health, social care, education and housing are going through processes of change. These processes of change are driven by contradictions that exist within and between organisations.

Within multi disciplinary team working, some of the contradictions that arise due to new expectations around developing a seamless service are becoming increasingly evident. How these contradictions will affect professional roles and boundaries is still to be seen. However, it is a brave person who will claim that nothing will change.

SECTION SIX: APPLYING THEORY TO PRACTICE

So far we have presented a range of theories in a way which should aid the reader to develop their knowledge and understanding. This section explores the way that theory can be applied to practice and should help the reader to begin to develop their understanding about how theory impacts on their daily practice.

Reading this section, you will learn more about:

- Eclecticism
- Formal and informal theory
- Theories *of* and theories *for* social work/social care

FURTHER READING

This handbook provides an introduction to the main theories of social care. For further more detailed information on the areas covered in this section, see the following:

- Beckett, C. (2006) *Essential Theory for Social Work Practice.* (London) SAGE.

- Fook, J. (2002) *Social Work: Critical Theory and Practice.* (London) SAGE.

- Payne, M. (2005) *Modern Social Work Theory.* Third Edition. (Basingstoke) Palgrave Macmillan.

- Thompson, M. (2002) *Theory and Practice in Human Services.* (Buckinghamshire) OU Press.

APPLYING THEORY TO PRACTICE

It is our view that social care staff are using theory in every aspect of their work. They may not always be able to name the theory, but they are using a range of ideas or theories in their work.

In Volume One, we introduced the concept of eclecticism which is essentially about using a range of different theories in a sort of pick and mix fashion. In our view, all social care professionals use an eclectic approach to the application of theory to practice. This is really the only effective way to work, in that no single theory provides a clear explanation about a service user's situation along with an appropriate and failsafe plan of action. The situations which social care staff deal with are complex and each one is unique. As such, service users have a right to expect an approach tailored to their particular situation which draws on a whole range of perspectives.

Types of Theory

Beckett (2006) separates theory into 'formal' theory and 'informal' theory. We have known some people use these terms inappropriately – formal theory being taken to mean theory which is presented more academically and informal theory taken to mean theory which is more accessible and understandable (and therefore not academic!). However, this is a misunderstanding. Formal theory is the theory that we have covered in this handbook (and there is more) – it is basically theory which can be named and traced back to a writer or an academic. Informal theory on the other hand, is the worker's own ideas about a situation. As this is often developed through experience – both practice experience and personal experiences, this type of 'theory' is also referred to as practice wisdom (Doel and Shardlow 1993). Beckett (2006) also refers to informal theory as "common knowledge".

Whilst Beckett categorises theory into formal and informal, other writers draw other distinctions. One common idea is that there are theories of social care/social work and theories for social care/social work. In straightforward terms, this means that there are theories about the way social care/social work is delivered which constitute theories of social care/social work – e.g.: task centred practice, crisis intervention etc. Theories for social care/social work are essentially theories which can explain situations, behaviours etc – such as behavioural approaches, systems theories etc.

Sibeon (1989) takes this idea further and proposes a three part distinction between theories:

- Theories of what social work does
- Theories of how to do social work
- Theories of the client's world

So with many different types of theory, a worker can call on different theories to help them in different aspects of their work role. For example a worker may call on some *formal theory about the client's world* to help them to understand what is happening for the service user, they may then draw on some *informal and formal theory* about *how to do social work* to plan their intervention. In presenting a case for resources to their manager, the worker may draw on all of these and some *formal theories* about *what social work does*. So in dealing with one service user's situation, a worker is likely to draw on a whole range of theory. Whether or not they can necessarily name the theory is another matter.

The range of types of theory a worker can draw on is illustrated in the following diagram.

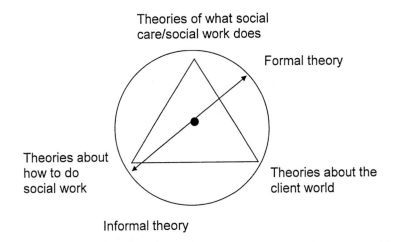

Really the nature and type of theory used is not really important, what is important is that you draw on a range of theories in your work, such that you can plan effectively and justify your actions. Using theory is theory is really part of the process of reflective practice and critical thinking. Beckett (2006) asserts that using theory in practice:

"means being clear about the ideas that guide your practice and thinking through how you are going to approach each task. Formal theory can augment and inform this process of thinking things through, but it cannot ever be a substitute for thinking for yourself."

(Beckett 2006: p.36)

As you develop your skills in applying theory in your work, remember that:

- No single theory ever has "the" answer.
- Different professionals may draw on different theories given the same presenting situation. There is no right or wrong approach – just boundaries of good practice.
- Theories of different types may be used at different points in intervention in a case/situation.
- Some theories may compliment each other, others may clash and may therefore not be appropriate to use together.
- An anti-oppressive approach is always vital – you should critically evaluate any theory you choose to use from an anti-oppressive standpoint.

HOW DO I APPLY THEORY TO MY PRACTICE? THEORY CIRCLES

If you are still unsure about whether you do apply theory to your practice, you might find it helpful to apply one of the following "theory circles".

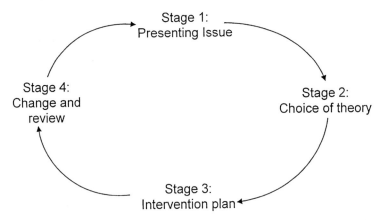

Stage 1:
Presenting Issue

Stage 2:
Choice of theory

Stage 3:
Intervention plan

Stage 4:
Change and
review

When a worker considers any presenting issue and decides on a plan of intervention, they have used a theory of some kind. They may not always be aware of it – but they have. For example, let's consider a situation where a worker is addressing a situation where a service user has behaviour which is viewed as challenging or difficult to manage. The theory circles which illustrate the different choices of theory open to the worker may illustrate the point:

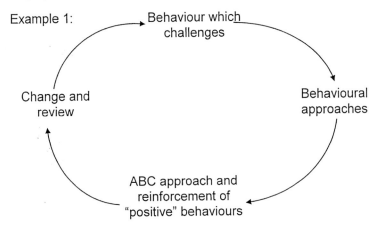

Example 1:

Behaviour which challenges

Behavioural approaches

ABC approach and reinforcement of "positive" behaviours

Change and review

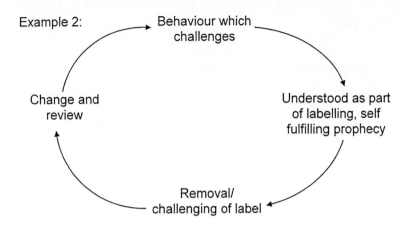

Example 2:

Behaviour which challenges

Understood as part of labelling, self fulfilling prophecy

Removal/ challenging of label

Change and review

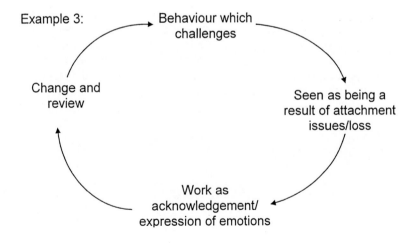

Example 3:

Behaviour which challenges

Seen as being a result of attachment issues/loss

Work as acknowledgement/ expression of emotions

Change and review

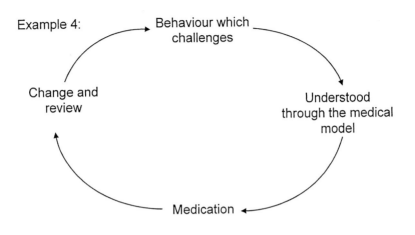

Example 4:

Behaviour which challenges

Understood through the medical model

Medication

Change and review

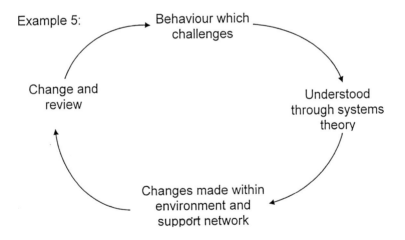

Example 5:

Behaviour which challenges

Understood through systems theory

Changes made within environment and support network

Change and review

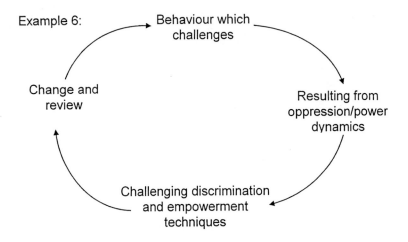

Example 6:

Behaviour which challenges

Resulting from oppression/power dynamics

Challenging discrimination and empowerment techniques

Change and review

Many more examples could be given! The basic point we are trying to illustrate is that whatever intervention is planned, is a result of the application of one theory or another. Many workers go straight from Stage 1 to Stage 3 in the "theory circle". Reflection and if necessary, some research and knowledge development should help the worker identify Stage 2 such that they can easily answer the dreaded question "and what theory are you using there?"

The following exercises may help workers – and particularly students to explore how they apply theory to their practice and to become more confident in this area.

- Apply the theory circle to one of your cases/pieces of work. Can you name the theory/theories you have used to plan your intervention?

- Use a reflective diary/learning log to reflect on situations/cases you found difficult/interesting. Try to identify any theories you have used, or that were used by others.

- Keep a separate sheet for theories you have used and discussed in your work. List each as you use it. Some repetition will probably occur. Can you see which theory you use most? Why do you subscribe to that one more than others?

APPENDIX ONE: CONTENTS OF A HANDBOOK OF THEORY: VOLUME ONE

Oppression and Anti-Oppressive Practice

The Value Base
Value Conflicts
Oppression and Anti-oppressive Practice
Who is Oppressed?
Types of Oppression
Mechanisms of Oppression
Social Imagery
Stereotyping
Labelling
Equality and Diversity

Human Development

Child Development
Erikson
Piaget
Vygotsky
Nature/Nurture Debate
Adult Development
Maslow's Hierarchy of Needs
Attachment Theory and Children
Attachment Theory and Adults
Identity
Identity Issues in Childhood
Identity Issues for Adults

Behavioural Theory

Classical Conditioning
Operant Conditioning
Social Learning/Role Modelling
Task Centred Work
Cognitive Behavioural Theory (CBT)
Behaviour that Challenges Services
Eclectisism

Power, Powerlessness and Empowerment

Power
Sources of Power
Care and Control
Powerlessness
Empowerment
Advocacy

Working With Stress and Distress

Stress and Stress Management
The Stress Vulnerability Model
Grief and Loss

Theories about Social Care Provision

The Medical Model
The Social Model
The Recovery Model
Group Work Theory
Social Role Valorisation
Service Accomplishments
Institutionalisation
Person Centred Care
Holistic Approach

Adult Learning

Principles of Adult Learning
Experiential Learning
Andragogy
Approaches to Learning
Learning styles
Dissonance
Reflective Practice

INDEX

REFERENCES

Argyris, C. (1964) *Integrating the Individual and the Organisation.* (New York) Wiley.

Atkinson, M., Wilkin, A., Scott, A., Doherty, P. and Kinder, K. (2002) *Multi-Agency Working: A detailed study.* (Slough) National Foundation for Education Research.

Barnardos (2006) *Family Group Conferences.* (online at www.barnardos.org.uk/familygroupconferences.htm - accessed 1.11.06)

Beckett, C. (2006) *Essential Theory for Social Work Practice* (London) SAGE.

Berne, E. (1978) *A Layman's Guide to Psychiatry and Psychoanalysis.* (London) Penguin.

Bion, W. (1962) *Learning from Experience* (London) Heinemann.

Blake, R. and Mouton, J. (1968) *The Managerial Grid, Key Orientations for Achieving Production Through People.* (Houston) Gulf Publishing Company.

Bradshaw, J. (1972) *The Concept of Social Need.* New Society 496. pp640-643

Bradshaw, W. (2003) *Use of single system research to evaluate the effectiveness of cognitive-behavioural treatment of schizophrenia.* British Journal of Social Work, 33, pp 885-899.

Brandon, D. (1997) *The Trick of Being Ordinary.* (Cambridge) Anglia Polytechnic.

Burford, G. and Hudson, J. (eds) (2000) *Family Group Conferencing: New directions in community-centred child and family practice* (New York) Aldine de Gruyter.

Burton, J. (ed) (1990) *Conflict: Human Needs Theory* (London) Macmillan.

Burton, J. (1990) *Conflict Resolution and Prevention.* (New York) St Martin's Press.

Caplan, G, (1965) *Principles of Preventative Psychiatry.* (London) Tavistock.

Carson, D. (1996) *Risking Legal Repercussions.* in Kemshall, H. and Pritchard, J, (ed) Good Practice in Risk Assessment and Risk Management (Volume 1). (London) Jessica Kingsley Publishing pp3-12.

Cm 5730 (2003) *The Victoria Climbié Inquiry.* Report of an Inquiry by Lord Lambing (online) at www.victoria-climbie-inquiry.org.uk/finreport/finreport.htm - accessed 18.10.06.

Coulshed, V. and Orme, J. (1998) *Social Work Practice: An Introduction.* (Basingstoke) Palgrave.

Cousins, N. (1989) *Head First: The Biology of Hope* (New York) E.P. Dutton.

Cross, W. (1971) *The negro to black conversion experience: towards the psychology of black liberation.* Black World 20, pp.13-27.

Cross, W. (1980) *Models of psychological nigrescence: a literature review.* In R. Jones (ed) Black Psychology (New York) Harper Row.

Cross, W. (1991) *Shades of Black: Diversity in African American Identity.* (Philadelphia) Temple University Press.

De Shazer, S. (1985) *Keys to Solution in Brief Therapy.* (New York) Norton.

Doel, M. and Marsh, P. (1992) *Task Centred Social Work.* (Aldershot) Ashgate.

Doel, M. and Shardlow, S. (1993) *Social Work Practice.* (Aldershot) Gower Publications.

Dominelli, L. (2002) *Feminist Theory.* In Davies, M. (Ed) The Blackwell Companion to Social Work. (Oxford) Blackwell.

Dutt, R. and Phillips, M. (2000) *Assessing black children in need and their families.* In Assessing Children in Need and their Families: Practice Guidance, Department of Health (London) The Stationery Office.

Engestrom, Y. (1999) *When the center does not hold: The importance of knotworking.* In S. Chaiklin (ed) Activity Theory and Social Practice (Aarhus) Aarhus University Press

Fayol, H. (1949) *General and Industrial Management.* (London) Pitman.

Fleming, I and Stenfert Kroese, B. (1993) *People with Learning Disability and Severe Challenging Behaviour – New Developments in Services and Therapy.* (Manchester) Manchester University Press.

Ford, P. and Postle, K. (2000) *Task centred practice and care management.* In P. Stepney and D, Ford (eds) Social Work Models, Methods and Theories (Dorset) Russell House Publishing Ltd.

Glendrinning, C., Hirst, M. and Harris, J. (2005) *Understanding and Measuring Personal Social Services Outputs Relating to Disabled Adults and Carers.* (York) SPRU University of York.

Harris, J., Foster, M., Jackson, K. and Morgan, H. (2005) *Outcomes for Disabled Service Users.* (York) SPRU. University of York.

Harris, T. (1970) *I'm OK – You're OK.* (London) Pan.

Higham, P. (2006) *Social Work. Introducing Professional Practice.* (London) Sage Publications.

Hylton, C. (1997) *Family Survival Strategies* (London) Exploring Parenthood.

Jacobs, M., (1999) *Psychodynamic Counselling in Action.* (London) SAGE.

Kemshall, H. (2002) *Risk Assessment and Management.* In Davies, M. (ed) The Blackwell Companion to Social Work (Oxford) Blackwell.

Limandri, B. and Sheridan, D. (1995) *The prediction of intentional interpersonal violence.* In J. Campbell (ed) Assessing Dangerousness: Violence by Sexual Offenders, Batterers and Child Abusers. (London) SAGE.

Macdonald, K. and Macdonald, G. (1999) *Perceptions of risk.* In Parsloe, P. (ed) Risk Assessment in Social Work and Social Care. (London) Jessica Kingsley.

Mayo, E. (1933, Reprint 2003) *The Human Problems of an Industrial Civilisation.* (London) Routledge.

McClelland, D. (1961) *The Achieving Society.* (Princeton) Van Nostrand.

McClelland, D. (1998) *Human Motivation.* (Cambridge) Cambridge University Press.

McGlone, F., Park, A. and Smith, K. (1998) *Families and Kinship.* (York) Jospeh Rowntree Foundation.

McGregor, D. (1957) *Proceedings of the Fifth Anniversary Convocation of the School of Industrial Management, the Human Side of Enterprise.* Massachusetts Institute of Technology.

McGregor, D. (1960) *The Human Side of Enterprise.* (New York) McGraw-Hill Book Company.

Messari, S. and Hallam, R. (2003) *CBT for psychosis: A qualitative analysis of clients experiences.* British Journal of Clinical Psychology, 42, pp. 171-188.

Milner, J. and O'Byrne, P. (1998) *Assessment in Social Work.* (Basingstoke) MacMillam.

Monahan, J. and Steadman, H. (1994) *Violence and Mental Disorder: Developments in Risk Assessment.* (Chicago) University of Chicago Press.

Morris, K. (1995) *Family Group Conferences: An Introductory Pack.* (London) Family Rights Group

Mullender, A. (2002) *Persistent oppressions: The example of domestic violence.* In Critical Practice in Social Work, R. Adams, L. Dominelli and M. Payne (Eds) (Basingstoke) Palgrave MacMillan.

National Institute for Mental Health in England (2003). *Inside Outside: Improving mental health services for black and minority ethnic communities in England.* (Leeds) Department of Health.

Neufeldt, A. (1990) *Celebrating Differences.* Journal of Practical Approaches to Developmental Handicap, 15, pp 3-6.

Orme, J. (2002) *Feminist Social Work.* In Social Work: Themes, Issues and Critical Debates. R. Adams, L. Dominelli and M. Payne (Eds) (Basingstoke) Palgrave/Open University.

Ossana, S., Helms, J. and Leonard, M. (1992) *Do 'womanist' identity attitudes influence college women's self esteem and perceptions of environmental bias?* Journal of Counselling and Develoment, 70, pp.402-408

Owusu-Bempah, K. (2002) *Culture, Ehtnicity and Identity.* In M. Davies (ed) The Blackwell Companion to Social Work (Oxford) Blackwell Publishing.

Owusu-Bempah, K. and Howitt, D. (1999) *Even their soul is defective.* The Psychologist 12.

Pam, A. (1995) *Biological psychiatry: science or pseudo science?* In C. Ross and A-Pam (eds) Pseudoscience in Biological Psychiatry: Blaming the Body (New York) Wiley.

Payne, M. (1997) *Modern Social Work Theory: A Critical Introduction.* (Basingstoke) Palgrave MacMillan.

Payne, M. (2005) *Modern Social Work Theory: 3rd edition* (Basingstoke) Palgrave MacMillan.

Perrow, C. (1967) *A Framework for the Comparative Analysis of Organisations.* American Sociological Review 32, pp.194-208.

Phillipson, C. (1998) *Reconstructing Old Age.* (London) SAGE

Pincus, A. and Minahan, A. (1973) *Social Work Practice: Model and Method,* (Itasca) Peacock.

Reid, W. (1978) *The Task Centred System.* (New York) Columbia University Press.

Reid, W. and Epstein, L. (ed) (1972) *Task Centred Practice* (New York) Columbia University Press.

Reid, W. and Shyne, A. (1969) *Brief and Extended Casework.* (New York) Columbia University Press.

Ridgeway, P. (2001) *Restorying Psychiatric Disability. Learning from first person recovery narratives.* Psychiatric Rehabilitation Journal, 24, pp 335-343.

Riessman, C. (2000) *Analysis of Personal Narratives.* In J. Gubrium and J. Holstein (Eds) Handbook of Interviewing. (New York) SAGE.

Sabin, T. (1990) *Toward the obsolescence of the schizophrenia hypothesis.* Journal of Mind Behaviour. 11. pp259-283.

Saleebey, D. (1996) *The strengths perspective in social work practice: extensions and cautions.* Social Work 41, pp296-305.

SCIE (2004) *Leading Practice: A Development Programme for First Line Managers.* (online at www.scie.org.uk/publications/leading practice/files/SCIE Participant's HB.pdf – accessed 1.11.06)

Selznick, P. (1949) *TVA and the Grass Roots.* (Berkley) University of California Press.

Sibeon, R. (1989) *Comments on the structure and form of social work knowledge.* Social Work and Social Sciences Review, 1 (1) pp.29-44.

Skinner, S. (1997) *Building Community Strengths: A Resource Book on Capacity Building.* (London) Community Development Foundation.

Smail, D. (1987) *Illusion and Reality: The Meaning of Anxiety* (London) Dent and Sons.

Smail, D. (1984) *Taking Care: An alternative to therapy* (London) Dent and Sons.

Smale, G., Tuson, G., Biehal, N. and Marsh, P. (1993) *Empowerment, Assessment, Care Management and the Skilled Worker.* (London) HMSO.

Smith, M. (1999) *Animation* [online www.infed.org/animate/b-animat.htm accessed 9.12.06]

Smith, M.K. (2006) *Community Work.* The Encyclopaedia of Informal Education [online www.infed.org/community/b-comwrk.htm - accessed 8.12.06]

Social Care Institute of Excellence (2003) *Learning and Teaching in Social Work Education: Assessment.* (London) SAGE.

Stenfert Kroese, B., Dewhurst, D. and Holmes, G. (2001) *Diagnoses and drugs: help or hindrance when people with learning disabilities have psychological problems?* British Journal of Learning Disabilities 29, p.27-33.

Stepney, P. and Ford, D. (eds) (2000) *Social work Models, Methods and Theories* (Dorset) Russell House Publishing.

Sutton, C. (1999) *Helping Families with Troubled Children.* (London) Wiley.

Tapsfield, R. (2003) *Family group conferences: family-led decision making.* Childright 195. p16-17.

Taylor, B. and Devine, D. (1993) *Assessing Needs and Planning Care in Social Work.* (London) Arena Press.

Thomas, D. (1983) *The Making of Community Work.* (London) Allen and Unwin.

Thompson, N. (2005) *Anti-Discriminatory Practice* Third Edition (Basingstoke) Palgrave.

Thompson, N. (2005) *Understanding Social Work. Preparing for Practice.* (Basingstoke) Palgrave Macmillan.

Topss England (2003) *National Occupational Standards for Social Work.* (Leeds) Topss England.

Roberts, A. (ed) (2005) *Crisis Intervention Handbook. Assessment, treatment and research.* (Oxford) Oxford University Press.

Vanier, J. (1988) *The Broken Body* (London) Darton, Longman and Todd Limited.

Walker, S. and Beckett, C. (2005) *Social Work Assessment and Intervention.* (Dorset) Russell House Publishing.

Warrington, P., Daniels, H., Edwards, A., Leadbetter, J., Martin, D., Brown, S. and Middleton, D. (2004) *Learning in and for Interagency Working: Conceptional Tensions in Joined up Practice.* Paper presented on the TLRP Annual Conference, Cardiff 2004.

Weber, M. (1947) *Theory of Social and Economic Organisation.* (New York) Free Press.

White, C., Holland, E., Marsland, D. and Oakes P. (2003) *The Identification of environments and cultures that promote the abuse of people with intellectual disabilities.* A review of the literature Journal of Applied Research in Intellectual Disabilities 16, pp.1-9.

Wilcox, D. (1994) *The Guide to Effective Partnership* (online www.partnerships.org.uk/guide - accessed 1.12.06).

Williams, P. (2006) *Social Work with People with Learning Difficulties* (Exeter) Learning Matters.

Wilson, V. and Pirrie, A. (2000) *Multidisciplinary Team-working* (Edinburgh) The Scottish Council for Research in Education.

Wolfensberger, W. (1988) *Common assets of mentally retarded people that are commonly not acknowledged.* Mental retardation, 26, pp 63-70.

Woodward, J. (1965) *Industrial Organisations: Theory and Practise.* (Oxford) Oxford University Press.

Younghusband, E. (1959) *Report of the Working Party on Social Workers in the Local Authority Health and Welfare Services.* (London) HMSO